Struggles in the Spiritual Life

Also by Timothy M. Gallagher, OMV
available from Sophia Institute Press:

Discernment of Spirits in Marriage

A Biblical Way of Praying the Mass

A Layman's Guide to the Liturgy of the Hours

Overcoming Spiritual Discouragement

Timothy M. Gallagher, OMV

Struggles in the Spiritual Life

Their Nature and Their Remedies

SOPHIA INSTITUTE PRESS
Manchester, New Hampshire

Sophia Institute Press
Box 5284, Manchester, NH 03108
1-800-888-9344

www.SophiaInstitute.com

Sophia Institute Press® is a registered trademark of Sophia Institute.

paperback ISBN 978-1-64413-630-0

ebook ISBN 978-1-64413-631-7

Library of Congress Control Number: 2022935608

First printing

Contents

Part 3
Forms of Dryness

Part 4
The Dark Night

Acknowledgments

I thank Charlie McKinney for perceiving the need for this book and inviting me to write it. Without his initiative, this book would never have been written. I express my warm thanks, once again, to Nora Malone for her invaluable aid in editing and preparing the book for printing; to Jean-Pierre Tetreault and Molly Rublee and all at Sophia Institute Press for their help in publishing the book; and to the readers who accompanied the writing and whose insights improved the book in many ways: Veronica Burchard, Larry Dwyer, James Gallagher, Cathie Macaulay, Father Bill Neubecker, OMV, and Elizabeth Valeri.

Struggles in the Spiritual Life

Introduction

A person says, "I'm struggling in my spiritual life. I don't understand what's happening, and I don't know what to do." Have you ever felt this in the past? Do you feel it now? I would imagine that, if you are reading this book, the answer to one or both questions is yes.

You are a person of faith. You love the Lord. You strive to serve the Lord in your married, single, priestly, or religious life. Your relationship with the Lord is important to you. God is central in your life. You are sincere. With good will, you try. But ... you struggle. You encounter difficulties. And you do not know why. Because you do not, you feel helpless. You do not see how to respond. And so, the struggle continues.

This book provides a presentation of these struggles. It identifies each and supplies its remedy. The book begins with the most basic struggles and continues to the most refined.

Each chapter presents one struggle. The first part of the chapter illustrates this struggle through an example. The characters portrayed—John, Beth, Paul, Julie, and the others—are not specific individuals by that name, but they reflect the experience of us all.[1] The second part of the chapter identifies the struggle and provides its remedies.

Part 1 of the book explores struggles that derive from non-spiritual (natural, human) factors. Part 2 reviews experiences of spiritual desolation with Saint Ignatius of Loyola as guide. Part 3 examines various forms of dryness. In Part 4, we consider the dark nights as Saint John of the Cross describes them.

This book is for dedicated Christians who struggle and who seek freedom from their struggles. Is there anyone to whom this does not apply, at least on occasion—or more frequently? Certainly, those who have spiritual directors will find their help greatly beneficial. Where spiritual direction is possible, I believe that both directors and those they assist will find this book useful. Others, perhaps many, may not have a spiritual director. If so, this book will be all the more valuable.

Certain chapters may speak to you in a special way. As you read one or another, you may find yourself saying, "Yes, I have experienced this! I have been (or am going) through this same struggle!" If so, that chapter and the remedies it proposes will be particularly helpful.

I write in my forty-second year of priesthood and religious life. All of those years with their personal experience and service to others have prepared this book. May it provide clarity, remove discouragement, and open the path to freedom.

Yes, this is a book about freedom! It is not primarily about struggles. It does treat of struggles, but only to find liberation from them. Jesus did not come that we might live in discouragement. He came to *set captives free* (Luke 4:18). May that freedom bless each day of our spiritual journeys.

---

[1] The one exception, after the prologue, is chapter 24, in which I cite the experience of Saint Teresa of Calcutta.

Prologue

With unimaginable love You looked upon Your creatures
within Your very Self, and You fell in love with us.

—Saint Catherine of Siena

On the morning of June 27, 1916, Raissa Maritain, wife of the philosopher Jacques Maritain, entered a time of prayer. She began with the Litany of the Sacred Heart and never moved beyond the first invocation. In her diary, she writes:

> At the first invocation, "Lord, have mercy," obliged to absorb myself, my mind arrested on the Person of the Father. Impossible to change the object. Sweetness, attraction, eternal youth of the heavenly Father. Suddenly, keen sense of his nearness, of his tenderness, of his incomprehensible love which impels him to demand our love, our thought. Greatly moved, I wept very sweet tears.... Joy of being able to call him Father with a great tenderness, to feel him so kind and so close to me.[2]

[2] Jacques Maritain, ed., *Raissa's Journal* (Albany: Magi, 1974), 35. In the original, "Lord, have mercy" is given in the Greek, "*Kyrie eleison.*"

Struggles in the Spiritual Life

One evening in May, author Julien Green returned to his lodg-
ings, took the Bible in hand, and began to read. He describes what
happened as he did so:

> In a corner of one's room when the day is closing, when the
> sounds of the city and of life die down a little, when in us lies the
> silence of twilight where God is perhaps more perceptible than
> at other moments — that is the time to open the Bible and listen
> to what it is going to say to us. To talk to God with a heart still
> warm with happiness. How He must love to be told that He is
> loved! And the more we tell Him so, the more He loves us.[3]

On an April day, Servant of God Elisabeth Leseur went to
Confession and then received Communion. She writes:

> Those moments were completely and supernaturally happy. I
> felt in myself the living presence of the Blessed Christ, of God
> Himself, bringing me an ineffable love; this incomparable Soul
> spoke to mine, and all the infinite tenderness of the Savior
> passed for an instant into me. Never will this divine trace be
> effaced. The triumphant Christ, the eternal Word, He who as
> man has suffered and loved, the one living God, took possession
> of my soul for all eternity in that unforgettable moment. I felt
> myself renewed to my very depths by Him, ready for a new life,
> for duty, for the work intended by His Providence. I gave myself
> without reserve, and I gave Him the future.[4]

[3] Julien Green, *Diary*, ed. Kurt Wolff (New York: Harcourt, Brace
& World, 1964), 287.
[4] Elisabeth Leseur, *My Spirit Rejoices: The Diary of a Christian Soul in
an Age of Unbelief* (Manchester, NH: Sophia Institute Press, 1996),
73-74.

Later in her journal, Elisabeth recounts a further experience of these sacraments:

> I had spent the morning in a state of extreme prostration and sadness; during the day I went to Confession, and I was at peace again; I seemed to be – and indeed I was – renewed by a strength other than my own. The feeling of forgiveness and spiritual renewal in the sacrament of Penance is a wonderful thing.
>
> And yesterday morning I went to Communion in the same peace and the same abandonment to God. I felt Christ Jesus truly living in me, and now I want to become different, to be wholly Christian, with all that that word means of forgetfulness of self, strength, serenity, and love.[5]

Saint Teresa of Avila says of Jesus that "whoever lives in the presence of so good a friend and excellent a leader, who went ahead of us to be the first to suffer, can endure all things. The Lord helps us, strengthens us, and never fails; He is a true friend."[6] Saint Bonaventure speaks of growth in prayer and affirms, "Here is such quiet and peace that the soul is, in a way, established in silence and is asleep, as if in Noah's Ark where tempests cannot reach."[7] Saint Thomas Aquinas writes that "nothing in this life can fulfill our desire, nor can anything created satisfy our desire. Only God satisfies, and He infinitely surpasses all else, whence our

---

[5] Ibid., 88.
[6] *The Collected Works of St. Teresa of Avila*, trans. Kieran Kavanaugh, OCD, and Otilio Rodriguez, OCD (Washington, DC: ICS Publications, 1976), vol. 1, 194.
[7] *The Works of Bonaventure*, vol. 1, *Mystical Opuscula*, trans. José de Vinck (Paterson, NJ: St. Anthony Guild Press, 1960), 78.

heart can only rest in God, as Augustine says, 'You have made us for yourself, Lord, and our heart is restless until it rests in You.'"[8]

Such examples and quotations could be multiplied at length. In their differing ways, all express the joy of the spiritual life, the peace that faith provides, the purpose, strength, hope, and energy that arise from our relationship with God. These blessings encourage us to live the spiritual life faithfully, and we are grateful for them.

We know, however, from experience that the spiritual life also includes struggles.

All who walk the spiritual journey undergo, in their individual ways, such struggles. Our spiritual tradition knows these struggles, explains their causes, and supplies their remedies. Such struggles lie within God's loving providence. Understood and faced well, they will not harm us. They will, on the contrary, lead to growth—the reason for which God permits them.

Struggles are not the heart of the spiritual life. God's love is—His deep, warm, faithful, and personal love for you. That is the center. That is the source of your joy. Because you know this, you love the spiritual life. And because you love it, you have begun to read this book.

We turn now to a wisdom that will protect this center and guide us into its richness.

---

[8] Thomas Aquinas, *Conferences on the Apostles Creed*, article 12, Corpus Thomisticum, https://www.corpusthomisticum.org/csv.html, author's translation. See the Office of Readings in the *Liturgy of the Hours*, Saturday of the Thirty-Third Week in Ordinary Time.

Part 1

Forms of Nonspiritual Desolation

1

"I Just Can't Pray"

John looked out the window. Streetlamps and windows in neighboring homes lit the darkness of the approaching night. His gaze dropped to the desk before him. There, a few inches before his hand, lay the Bible. Normally at this time, he read from it for ten to fifteen minutes. Tonight, nothing in him wanted to do so.

He thought back to the beginning of the day. For months now, he had attended daily Mass before work. This morning, he had barely gotten himself to church and had paid little attention to the Mass, just wanting it to end.

Then John recalled the commute home from work. Usually, he would play a Rosary app as he drove. But this day the same pattern held: he had felt no desire to pray the Rosary and had listened to music instead.

Seated at his desk in the silence of his room, John grew troubled. Days like today were becoming more common. He was losing something. Something had to change.

A week later:

John opened the gate, approached the rectory, rang, and waited. A minute later, the door opened, and Father Reed welcomed him.

John returned his greeting, crossed the vestibule, and entered the parlor, where he and Father Reed always met. They sat by the windows, their chairs facing each other. The afternoon sun filled the room, and subdued sounds of traffic created a quiet background. As usual, when he met Father Reed, John felt his heart lift.

For a few minutes, they spoke of John's family, his wife, Jennie, and their children. Then Father Reed offered a prayer. When he finished, he settled in his chair, smiled warmly, and prepared to listen. This was John's cue to speak.

For a moment, John gazed at Father Reed. His frailty was evident, and he looked all of his seventy-five years. But his heart had not changed. His physical sufferings had deepened the goodness and care for others that had long characterized his priesthood.

"When I last came, four weeks ago," John began, "I was happy with my prayer. It seemed to be growing, and I felt that I was growing closer to God. Daily Mass, when I could get to it, made a real difference in the day. Somehow, it felt alive. The readings spoke to me, and I sensed the Lord's presence when I received Communion. The Mass helped me to be more patient at work, a better husband and father, and ... just happier. I liked listening to the Rosary app when I drove home from work, and I liked my prayer at the end of the day, the time I spent reading the Bible and making my examen. This prayer brought Jennie and me closer, and we both loved it."

"Yes, I remember you telling me about this," said Father Reed.

"But now I feel like I just can't pray. It's frustrating. I don't know what's going on, and I don't like it."

"Can you tell me more about what's happening?" Father Reed asked.

"Well, I don't feel God's closeness in the same way. I go to daily Mass because I want to be faithful, but it doesn't energize me the way it used to. I try to pray the Mass, but my mind wanders, and I feel bad about that. And to be honest, I don't really want to pray the Rosary during the commute. Some days I don't. I pray before retiring, but it's simply to get it done. I'm tired, and what I really want is to go to bed and sleep." John smiled a bit wanly, "Not a very pretty picture, is it?"

"What are your days like now?" Father Reed asked.

"That's a good question," John answered. "The days are full. Work has been busy. Jennie has had the flu recently, and she has needed extra help with the children. Actually, now that I talk about it, life has been pretty much nonstop for several weeks." He paused and looked at Father Reed. "To be really honest, though," he said sheepishly, "it isn't just that. Football season has started, and I've been staying up at night watching the games, even reruns when there is no game that evening. Then I watch other things, or I go on the phone. Sometimes it's quite late before I get to bed."

"John, several times now you've talked about being tired, wanting to sleep, and getting to bed at night. How is your energy these days?" Father Reed asked.

"Not good. I'm always tired. Things irritate me more easily, and everything weighs more. Also, when I don't get enough sleep, I don't exercise. And when I don't exercise, I don't eat properly either."

"Do you think that your prayer, your tiredness, and the demands on your energy are in any way linked?"

John smiled wryly and said, "It seems pretty obvious, doesn't it? Yes, I'm sure that they are."

"Can you think of anything else that has changed in recent weeks that might make prayer harder?"

John reflected for a moment. "No, not really," he said, "I think it comes down to being more tired."

"If that's so, what do you think might help you pray better?"

John laughed. "You don't miss much, do you? If I got more sleep at night, it would help."

"That sounds right to me," Father Reed said, "and I don't think we should assume deeper problems until we eliminate this one. The body is important in prayer, and proper care of it helps a great deal in the spiritual life. In a way, it's encouraging that there is no serious problem in your relationship with the Lord and your prayer. Most likely, you just need a better rhythm of life. Because work and family are making more demands now, managing your time is even more important."

John smiled. "I'll give it a try," he said, "and I'll let you know how it goes."

∾

Yes, the spiritual life is easier when we take wise care of the body. If you struggle in the spiritual life, ask first: How is my physical energy? Do I get enough sleep? Do I exercise sufficiently? Does my diet sustain my energy? If the answers are positive, you may presume that spiritual struggles, should you experience them, arise from a different cause. But it is wise to ask these questions before you presume this.

Sometimes, life simply makes demands on our energy. If John's pace at work increases still more, if his wife's illness grows more serious and long-lasting, if he himself faces physical issues, if the children's needs increase, and the like, then his energy for prayer will be less. God never asks the impossible! John, or any one of us in similar circumstances, can only do our best to care for our energy. Such expenditures of energy, accepted out of love for our vocation—in this case, marriage and fatherhood—bring us closer to God, though our prayer may be more tired.

Even in such situations, however, God asks us to care for the body as best we can. And this will bless our prayer.

Saint Teresa of Avila writes, "Take care, then, of the body for the love of God, because at many times the body must serve the soul."[9] Take care of the body—*why*? For what reason? "For the love of God." The soul needs the body. Prudent care of the body resolves many struggles in the spiritual life.

Like you, I have a daily rhythm of prayer. I chose it, and I adhere to it because I know its benefits. But some days—and I doubt I am alone in this!—I feel that "today, I just can't do it." What often solves this is exercise. I exercise, and then I am ready to pray. I want to pray. The problem never was lack of desire for prayer; it was lack of attention to a need of my physical humanity.

Years ago, when I made the Ignatian Spiritual Exercises, the Jesuit who guided my group said, "For many of us, having a spiritual life comes down to one thing: getting to bed on time." Wise words!

In Ignatian terms, John's issue is *nonspiritual* (that is, natural, human, physical) *desolation* (that is, heaviness of heart) caused by a diminishment of physical energy.[10] The remedy is evident.

---

[9] *Life*, XI, 16, quoted in Augustin Poulain, SJ, *The Graces of Interior Prayer* (London: Routledge and Kegan Paul Limited, 1950), 140.

[10] Timothy M. Gallagher, OMV, *The Discernment of Spirits: An Ignatian Guide to Everyday Living* (New York: Crossroad, 2005), 60-61.

2

"I Try to Pray, but I'm So Discouraged"

First e-mail from Beth to her sister:

> *I'm in the apartment now, and I guess that concludes the move. On Monday, I'll begin working in the clinic. I think it will be good. I'll let you know how it goes. Thank you, again, for helping me get settled here.*

Second e-mail from Beth to her sister, a week later:

> *First impressions of the clinic are positive. The setup for physical therapy is good, and overall, my initial contact with the others has been too. One of them, Susan, is helping me get integrated here. I say "overall," because I'm less sure of how Susan and I are going to get along.*

A year later:

Beth rang the rectory doorbell and waited as Father Reed approached the door. Her workday as a physical therapist had just ended, and, like John, she had come to speak with Father Reed.

He opened the door, smiled, greeted Beth, and invited her into the parlor. They spoke for a few minutes. Then Father Reed offered a prayer and waited for Beth to begin. She looked tired and discouraged, and he was not surprised when her first words addressed this heaviness.

"You know, Father," Beth said, "that I come here straight from work. Something I've mentioned before happened again today, and it always leaves me depressed."

"Tell me," said Father Reed.

"It's Susan again," Beth replied, "my coworker at the clinic. I've told you how difficult I find her. She's rough and overbearing, or at least I find her so. But it's not even that. It's her constant criticism of my work. I don't know why, but she never stops belittling me.

"Yesterday, I was working with an elderly man who had back pain. It was his first visit, and I was trying to identify his issues in order to formulate a plan for treatment. We were out in the large room, and I had him on the treadmill. I asked him just to walk normally, and I watched how he was doing. Susan managed to pass by several times and always with a scornful look that said, 'You're getting this all wrong. You don't know what you're doing. You won't be able to help him.' It really, really bothers me when she does this, and I start to get nervous."

Beth paused for a moment. "This has been going on for a long time," she said, "and it wears on me. When I get home after a day like that, I try to pray, but I'm too discouraged. I wind up watching movies or reading the feed on Facebook, getting emptier and more depressed all the time. Sometimes, I call Maureen. I know that will turn into gossip and leave me empty too, but I do it because I feel so alone. Some evenings, I just don't pray at all."

Beth looked at Father Reed and said, "To be honest, Father, when it's like this, I find it hard to come here. It feels as though, even though you're too kind to say it, inside you're thinking, 'Won't she ever get her act together? How long will I have to put up with this?' "

Father Reed was silent for a moment. Then he said, "Your relationship with Susan sounds difficult. Have you found anything that helps you with it?"

"Nothing that really helps," replied Beth. "I've often wondered why her criticism hits me so hard. I know that I'm a competent therapist, but when Susan or anyone like her attacks me in that way, I feel defenseless. It's as if there is already self-doubt in me, and she touches it in a way that hurts. Father, how do you pray when you're feeling so bad? What do you do? And it isn't just prayer. If affects everything."

Father Reed thought and then asked, "Beth, have you ever talked to anyone about this?"

"What do you mean?"

"I mean about this struggle you're describing and how it affects everything."

"No, not really."

"It must be hard to carry this alone."

"Yes, it is. And it doesn't help that when I get home from work, I'm alone in the apartment. I don't want to do anything, and I just vegetate. And when I feel like this, often I don't sleep well either."

Father Reed paused, and then said, "It's just a thought, but I wonder if a conversation or two with a good Catholic counselor might help."

"Do you know, Father," Beth replied, "I've wondered about that myself. Do you think it might be good to try that?"

"It might be worth considering. You could think about it and maybe pray about it as well. In the meantime, do what you can to resist the discouragement. Could you try to do healthy things when you feel this way? Things like exercising, calling a friend or a family member, or spending time on a project you enjoy."

"I can try. But it's not easy when I feel this way."

Father Reed nodded his understanding. "Do what you can," he said. "And this is important: tell Jesus what you're feeling. Let Him be with you as you go through it. He doesn't want you to be alone. And you are not alone. He is with you. He loves you, and He wants to share this with you. Here is a Gospel verse that might help: Matthew 11:28, "Come to me, all you who labor and are burdened, and I will give you rest." Let Him say these words to you when you feel discouraged."

"Okay, I'll try." Beth answered. "It helps just to talk about it."

∞

If the spiritual life is easier when we care for the body, it is also easier when we care for our hearts—our emotions, our feelings, the psychological dimension of our humanity. In Ignatian terms, Beth is experiencing a *nonspiritual* (natural, human, psychological) *desolation* arising from a depletion of emotional energy. Said more simply, Beth is depressed, and this is affecting her spiritual life. She is, as she says, "too discouraged to pray."

Father Reed is aware of this. Beth's response to Susan, while it does say something about Susan, reveals a vulnerability in Beth herself. The depth of her discouragement—when she knows she is a competent therapist—highlights a self-doubt that precedes her relationship with Susan and is touched by it. Father Reed, as a spiritual director, wisely does not attempt himself to help Beth with a psychological issue. Rather, he suggests that she consider appropriate help with this. Father Reed has planted a seed in Beth's mind. She will reflect and pray about counseling, and if she feels ready, she may begin this process. If she does, the healing of an emotional vulnerability will most likely lighten her spiritual struggles as well.

Certainly, not every emotional struggle (nonspiritual desolation) requires counseling. For Beth, who says that her discouragement "affects everything," that it leaves her "too discouraged to pray," that she "winds up watching movies or reading the feed on Facebook, getting emptier and more depressed all the time," that she "just vegetates," and that she finds sleep difficult, the discouragement appears significant enough for counseling to help.

A certain amount of discouragement, however, is found in every life. Things do not always go well. Physical problems, financial burdens, family troubles, and the like present themselves. At such times, prayer may become more difficult. These situations call for both human and spiritual resources: time with family and friends, exercise, rest, service to others; prayer, Mass, Eucharistic Adoration, Scripture, the Rosary, the Liturgy of the Hours, spiritual reading, a group in the parish. These means are available to all. If Beth and you and I apply them in time of discouragement, our discouragement will lighten.

When we respond well to discouragement, our spiritual lives benefit greatly. A classic principle underlies this: "*gratia supponit perficitque naturam*," that is, "grace presupposes nature and perfects it." God's supernatural life in our souls—His grace—presupposes our humanity and elevates it. Therefore, whatever strengthens our humanity, whatever assists our physical and psychological well-being, opens us more fully to God's grace. If Beth and you and I care properly for our physical and emotional humanity, our spiritual lives will grow easier.

Do you struggle in your prayer, your vocation, your service of God? The answer, at times, will be yes. When you do, consider the helpful questions in this chapter and the previous one. Not all spiritual struggles arise from physical or emotional factors. We do well, however, not to overlook these when faced with spiritual burdens.

3

"I Can't Go On"

From Paul's journal, January 10:

> I find that going to daily Mass when I can makes a real dif-
> ference. I'll try to do this at least a few times a week.

From Paul's journal, March 15:

> I've begun using the app with the daily readings for Mass,
> and I like it. When I can't get to Mass, I'll spend a few
> minutes with the readings.

From Paul's journal, May 3:

> This daily prayer helps me face the day with more peace, and
> I have more patience with my students. I also sense some-
> thing new in my relationship with Rose and the children. I
> know that she's happy about it, and I am too.

From Paul's journal, June 15:

> Father Bauer asked if I'd consider being a Eucharistic
> Minister for Masses on Sunday. I'm willing to do it, and

Rose supports this. I think it will bring me closer to the Lord. I was happy to be asked. I feel as though my faith is the most alive it's ever been.

From Paul's journal, July 7:

Rose and I spoke about my getting a master's degree. We both think it's time that I start. It would give me more credibility as a teacher and would mean a better salary, which we will need for the family as it grows. It would also make me a better teacher. Since I'll have to do it part time, it could take three to four years. I'd like to get it done sooner than that, and I'll do my best.

From Paul's journal, October 14:

Life has gotten busy: full days at the high school and then evening classes for the degree, with the related reading. I like the material, and I see how it will help me as a teacher.

From Paul's journal, November 18:

It's getting harder to keep up with everything. I'm probably taking too many courses, but I want to get this done, not just for my sake but for the family, so that things can get back to normal.

From Paul's journal, April 23:

I'm dragging every day. I don't want to go to another class or read another textbook. I used to look forward to teaching, but now I have to make myself do it, and I'm not teaching as well as before. I know the students sense it. Everything feels like a burden. It all comes down to this: I'm tired — really tired. I've never felt like this before. I know Rose is worried. I've also noticed that I haven't mentioned prayer in this journal for several months, and it used to be the main thing, the reason why I started the journal. Rose thinks I should speak with Father Reed at the parish. I don't know him well, but I like what I've seen of him. I know others talk to him, and probably I should too.

Paul and Father Reed sat in the parlor. Paul introduced himself, and after a prayer, Father Reed encouraged Paul to speak.

Paul described his growth in prayer over recent years and the joy this brought him and his family. Father Reed listened as Paul recounted the various steps of this growth. Paul then told him that prayer had become less frequent and less fruitful in the past months — since life had grown so busy with family, teaching, and the degree. He described his packed, nonstop days as he strove to meet his obligations and finish his studies. He stopped speaking and looked at Father Reed.

"Paul, how have you been feeling lately?" Father Reed asked.

Paul did not reply immediately. Father Reed waited.

"Do you want a really honest answer?" Paul paused. "I know that you do," he said, "but it's just that I've never put this into words before, not even with Rose. What I feel scares me."

"Can you describe it?"

"I get up tired. I don't want to face the day. I don't want to pray or help in the parish. Even being present to my wife and children

feels like a burden. And this scares me. I love them, but that's
what it feels like now: a burden. I drag myself to the school, and
I'm just glad when the day is over—or I would be, except that it
means going to class in the evening and doing the assignments. My
sleep is poor. I'm not exercising. I just try to get through the day,
and I'm glad when it's over. I could say more, but I think you get
the picture. I can sum it up this way: I'm tired, I'm discouraged,
I feel like I can't go on, and I don't see the way out. How do you
even pray when you feel like this? As you see, my spiritual life is
going badly too."

"Paul, that's an honest answer, and I'm glad that you were able
to say it. It's a first step toward finding your way forward." Then
he asked, "As you've heard yourself describe your situation, how
does it sound to you?"

"Not too good, and certainly not sustainable." Paul thought for a
moment and said, "I wonder, is this what they mean by 'burnout'?"

Father Reed nodded, "Yes, I'd say that fits. And it's encouraging
that you can name it. Now you can start to change things." Then
he asked, "What do you think might help?"

Once more, Paul hesitated. "It's hard for me to say this, but
I probably have to slow the pace of studies for the degree. That
will allow me to rest more and have more energy for everything:
teaching, family, classes, and prayer."

"I think that's a good place to start," Father Reed said. "I think
it would be good to speak openly with Rose about this. It might
also help to meet with your doctor, get a physical, and see what
advice he gives."

∞

Paul's struggle, like John's and Beth's, is on the natural, human
level: his physical and emotional energies are depleted—in this case,

through excessive expenditure of those energies. The difference between Paul's situation and John's and Beth's is one of degree: his energies are far more diminished than theirs, and his situation is correspondingly more serious. With good intentions but without prudence, Paul has overextended himself and paid the price.

In all likelihood, Paul's conversation with Father Reed will prove a turning point. Accepting his limits, he will establish a healthier rhythm of life. As he does, a proper balance will return, and the heaviness will correspondingly lift. Paul will no longer feel that he "can't go on," and his love for his family and his teaching will be felt as before. His spiritual life will resume as before, and the former growth will likely continue.

In Ignatian terms, Paul experiences a severe instance of nonspiritual desolation with consequent harm to his spiritual life. When he applies appropriate nonspiritual remedies, his spiritual struggles will lessen.

In this and the preceding chapters, we have explored spiritual struggles arising from physical and psychological factors. As we have seen, the solution lies in suitable physical and psychological remedies. What, however, of struggles arising from specifically spiritual sources? What might these struggles be, and how can we best respond to them? We will begin now to address these questions.

Part 2

Forms of Spiritual Desolation

4

"I Can't See"

First e-mail from Julie to her friend Emily:

*It's the end of the day, and the house is quiet. All three
children are sleeping, and Bob is finishing a project for work
tomorrow. You asked how things are going. Spiritually, these
past months have been good. Prayer seems more alive, and I
find that Mass, when I can get to it during the week, makes
a difference. The greater peace I feel also helps me relate
better to Bob and the children. I'm grateful for your advice
about how to pray and about ways to come closer to God.
So, this is an end-of-the-day thank-you.*

Second e-mail from Julie to Emily, three weeks later:

*Yes, I still feel the Lord's closeness, and I'm thankful. Do
you know: when you first suggested that I pray with Scripture
for ten minutes every day, I thought I'd never be able to do
it. I'd never read the Bible, and you know how I can get
enthused about things but not follow through. However, I've
been doing it for three months now, and with the book you*

suggested, it works well. I actually look forward to that time every morning and miss it when I can't get it. When that happens, I find a time later in the day to do it.

Third e-mail from Julie to Emily, one month later:

Prayer continues to be a blessing, and I'm beginning to think that, this time, I may really persevere. I might even take further steps to grow in prayer! At least, I find myself thinking about it. Bob and the children also sense a difference in me, and we love what's happening in our family.

Fourth e-mail from Julie to Emily, three months later:

I know it's been a long time since I've replied to your e-mail, and I imagine that you've been worrying. I don't know what's happened. All that peace, that joy, that gratitude, and that sense of growth I talked about in earlier e-mails – it isn't the same anymore. The hard thing is that I don't understand this. I try to pray, and I just feel confused. To be honest, because it's gotten harder, sometimes I don't pray. What's going on? Was that joy I felt earlier real? If it was, why don't I feel it now? It's easy to get discouraged.

Fifth e-mail from Julie to Emily, a week later:

Thank you for your encouragement, but I still feel disheartened. I thought I was making such good progress and that this time I really would persevere. Now, I'm not so sure. How many times have I tried to grow spiritually, and you know how often I've given up. The best word I can use for it is "darkness": I'm confused, I don't see clearly, I don't understand what's happening in my life of prayer, and I feel like it will get worse. What do you do in times like this? How do you make sense out of this? Why does God allow it? Things seemed so good before. Now they have gotten heavier and darker, and I don't know why. Can't anyone help me? The danger is that I'll just give up.

Julie raises important questions. May I ask: Have you ever felt the spiritual heaviness, the darkness, that Julie now feels? Have you ever raised questions like hers? If so, one thing must be said immediately: *there is no shame* in experiencing such darkness, such heaviness in the spiritual life. Julie is undergoing a tactic of the enemy that Ignatius calls spiritual desolation.

By *enemy*, Ignatius intends Satan and his associated fallen angels, together with the wound of concupiscence—a legacy of original sin—and harmful influences around us in the world. By *spiritual desolation*, he intends a heaviness of heart (and so, *desolation*) on the level of our relationship with God (and so, *spiritual*).

Julie experiences one form of such spiritual desolation, a form that Ignatius calls "darkness of soul."[11] In such spiritual desolation, a burden, a confusion, a heaviness—a darkness—enters our prayer and our efforts to love God. A feeling that this will worsen may accompany this darkness.

---

[11] In his *Spiritual Exercises*, no. 317, Ignatius lists the various forms of spiritual desolation that we are examining in part 2 of this book. Having indicated the source of his words, I will not repeat the reference each time.

As Julie's experience indicates, there is nothing dramatic about this tactic of the enemy. She and we should not be surprised if, after a time of joy in the Lord, the enemy attempts to discourage us with such darkness of heart. This is a common, ordinary, undramatic tactic of the enemy in those who, like Julie, seek to grow spiritually. Obviously, if not detected and not resisted, it will harm us.

An efficacious remedy is at hand. If Julie—either because she is experienced enough herself or with the help of a competent spiritual person—is *aware* of this darkness, can *identify* it as the discouraging lie of the enemy that it is, and firmly *rejects* it, no harm will come to her.

The enemy's lie says, "Look how badly things are going! You are confused. You can't see clearly. You are regressing. And things will only get worse." No! For months, Julie has prayed faithfully and sought to grow. She is simply—again, there is no shame in this—experiencing a tactic of the enemy: a spiritual desolation that the enemy hopes will impede her growth.

In fact, if the enemy brings this desolation to Julie, it is precisely *because she is growing*. Not only that: by identifying and rejecting this tactic of the enemy, Julie will be further strengthened to love and serve God. The same is true of our spiritual lives.

How, then, do we reject spiritual desolation? Ignatius offers an effective answer in his fourteen rules for discernment (*Spir. Ex.*, 313-327). We will begin to explore his teaching here and continue in the next chapters.

Julie will reject this spiritual desolation, first of all, if she refuses to omit her daily prayer on account of it. This is Ignatius's classic rule 5: "In time of desolation, never make a change." In time of spiritual desolation, *never make a change* to anything you had planned to do in your spiritual life before that desolation began. Julie describes the heaviness she feels and tells Emily, "To be honest, because it's gotten harder, sometimes I don't pray." If she recalls Ignatius's counsel and refuses to omit her prayer on account of this darkness, Julie will already begin to defeat the enemy. The burden will not grow, and its hold will weaken. Light will return.

If you remain firm in such times, you, too, will find the darkness pass.

5

"I've Lost My Peace"

From Paul's journal, six months after the last entry cited (see chapter 3):

> *I continue to feel better, with more energy and improved spirits. It was hard to follow Father Reed's advice and slow the pace of studies, but he was right. The master's will take longer, but I have recovered my love for teaching, and matters in the family are going better. It's been good, also, to look forward to prayer again rather than just getting through it because I was so tired.*

From Paul's journal, three weeks later:

> *I've begun listening to Saint Francis de Sales's* Introduction to the Devout Life *during the commute home, and I find it uplifting. I've never seen so clearly that God calls me, a layman, a husband, a father, and a teacher, to be holy, and that this is possible. Saint. Francis's words return when I pray in the morning and at Mass, and they give me renewed desire for God. They bring me peace.*

Struggles in the Spiritual Life

From Paul's journal, one month later:

> I've started going to confession more regularly, and I like it.
> I feel a unique kind of peace after confession. Sometimes,
> it has to do with the priest's words to me, and I appreciate
> them. But there is a deeper level of peace from the sacrament
> itself: a sense of rightness, of no obstacles between me and
> the Lord, of doors wide open between us, of even small bur-
> dens lifted. I've come to love the final words, "Go in peace."

From Paul's journal, five weeks later:

> I'm not sure what's happening, but the peace I've felt in my
> relationship with God is less now. It bothers me. I wonder
> what's going on.

From Paul's journal, three weeks later:

> It's hard to settle down to pray. I'm troubled and restless when I
> try. I look at my watch, waiting for the time to end. Why? Am
> I trying too hard again? No, not as before, when I was pushing
> the studies. Maybe Introduction to the Devout Life isn't
> the best book for me? Maybe I'm not approaching confession
> right? Am I omitting things I should mention in confession? All
> I know is that I don't have the peace I used to have.

From Paul's journal, two weeks later:

> I haven't stopped praying, but I still have that sense of
> restlessness and turmoil. I keep asking myself what I'm doing
> wrong, and I don't find answers. Do I need to try harder?

Or am I trying too hard and need to try less? Is this trouble
a sign that I am regressing spiritually? I certainly had more
peace before. I don't know what to think, and I'm starting to
get discouraged.

∞

We see no sign that Paul is doing anything wrong. He is faithful.
He does not allow this turmoil, this lack of peace, to stop him
from praying. Still, it does trouble him.

Paul is experiencing a form of spiritual desolation that Ignatius
terms a "disturbance of soul." When people love the Lord, Ignatius
says, and rejoice in the peace this brings, the enemy may attempt
to undermine that peace by troubling them. Elsewhere, Ignatius
describes this spiritual disturbance as the enemy's "war against the
peace" these people experience.[12]

Note that the enemy does not, at this point, tempt Paul to
anything sinful. He seeks rather to diminish and even eliminate
Paul's peace, replacing it with trouble of heart. Again, there is no
shame in experiencing this or similar tactics of the enemy. It is
simply what happens when we live the spiritual life in a fallen but
redeemed and loved world.

As with Julie, Paul will not be harmed if he is aware of, identifies, and rejects the enemy's spiritual desolation. Obviously, if
Paul—or any one of us—does *not* identify and reject this tactic of
the enemy, it will cause harm.

What, then, of Paul's questions? Is his disturbance a sign
that he is doing something wrong? That he is trying too hard?

---

[12] Ignacio Iparraguirre, SJ, ed., *Directoria Exercitiorum Spiritualium*
(1540–1599) (Rome: Monumenta Historica Societatis Iesu, 1955),
72. The quote is found in Ignatius's *Autograph Directory*, no. 12.

Trying too little? That he is regressing? The answer to all these questions appears to be no. In Paul's journal, we see no sign of regression—quite the contrary. Most probably, precisely because Paul is progressing so well, the enemy induces this "disturbance of soul" and "war against peace" in an attempt to hinder his progress.

How does Paul and how do we reject such disturbance from the enemy? As already said, the first need is to make no changes, to relinquish nothing of the spiritual program we have in place. On the contrary, Ignatius says (rule 6), employ these four spiritual means:

Prayer of petition: When troubled in this way, turn to God, to the Persons of the Trinity, to Mary, to your angel, to your special saints, and ask for help, mindful of Jesus's promise that such prayers will be answered (Matt. 7:7).

Meditation: When disturbed, call to mind biblical verses that strengthen you—verses that speak to your heart—and pray with them; reflect on truths of faith (God's love, power, grace, closeness, providence) that will hearten you; remember past times of struggle and how God has always brought you safely through them.

Examination: Ask, "What am I feeling?" To identify this disturbance as a tactic of the enemy, as spiritual desolation, is enormously liberating. Ask also, "How did this begin?" If you can pinpoint the origin of the disturbance—when that interaction happened, when you received that e-mail, when he or she said that, or similar—you will find it easier to determine its remedy.

Suitable penance: Ignatius speaks of "some suitable way of doing penance," that is, gestures of courage, no matter how small, that help us seek God's grace in the struggle. Such gestures are the direct opposite of flight from desolation through turning to gratifications that will not resolve it—the Internet, social media, empty conversation, unnecessary food, and the like. Rather, in small but courageous ways, stand your ground: reach out to one who needs your help, answer the phone call of that family member or friend who waits to hear from you, render a small service to another person, or try another such "suitable penance."

If Paul, and we with him, apply these spiritual means when our hearts are disturbed by the enemy, the resulting benefit is evident. These four means will help us reject every form of spiritual desolation the enemy may bring.

Finally, we may note a quality of spiritual desolation, a part of its lie, that will often be present when the enemy seeks to discourage us through such desolation. In his desolation, Paul feels that "things are going badly and are likely to get worse" in his spiritual life. If we are not aware of, do not identify, and do not reject spiritual desolation, it will claim power to predict our spiritual future—and always in a dark key. Not only that, but it will also attempt to interpret our spiritual past—again, always in a dark key.

The desolation (that is, the enemy in time of desolation) will say to Paul: "Look at how you struggle in your spiritual life! Look at how poorly you pray. And it's only going to get worse [claim of power to predict the future]. You'll never be much of a man of prayer. And you know what else? You've never prayed well [claim of power to interpret the past]." No! Paul is a man who loves the

Lord, who has lived this relationship at length, and who even now is growing in it. Such promptings are simply lies from the "liar and father of lies" (John 8:44). To recognize this awakens a wonderful freedom to love and serve the Lord.

6

"How Can I Be Drawn to Such Things?"

Beth parked the car, walked to the entrance of her building, and rode the elevator to her apartment. It had been a tiring day at work, and tension with Susan had burdened her throughout. Beth prepared her supper, ate, washed up, and prepared to pray. The darkness of a cold winter evening enveloped the building.

Normally at this time Beth, prayed Evening Prayer from the Liturgy of the Hours. It was a welcome moment of prayer, a bridge between the pressure of the day and the more relaxed evening. With Father Reed's help, she was learning the examen prayer, a review of the day with the Lord, and she prayed this after Evening Prayer.

But this night, Beth felt no desire to pray. She was tired and discouraged. She felt alone. God and his love seemed distant. Something in her did not want to pray. Prayer could wait.

Beth took the phone and called Maureen, her coworker at the clinic. Beth knew where the conversation would lead: their talk would soon lead to gossip and criticism of others in the clinic. Beth was ready to hear criticism of Susan, and Maureen did not disappoint her. The call ended forty-five minutes later.

Beth's breviary with Evening Prayer was still at hand. But now, she had even less desire to pray it. She turned on the television. For the next hour, she watched a show about emotional struggles, personal conflicts, and broken relationships. The show left her depressed. She went to the refrigerator and chose food that she knew was not good for her. Feeling as she did, Beth guessed that this would not be her last trip to the refrigerator. It was not. As she ate, she went on social media and spent an hour there, feeling increasingly empty.

Now it was late, and still she had not prayed. Reluctantly, Beth opened the breviary and prayed Evening Prayer rapidly, simply to get it done. Her examen prayer was also quick and superficial. Even so, those few minutes of prayer helped a little. Beth retired unhappy and ashamed of how she had spent her evening.

∞

From Beth's journal, before retiring:

> *Why do I do this to myself? What is wrong with me? I knew even before I called Maureen that speaking with her would not help. I knew that prayer would. But I just felt too tired and too discouraged to pray. I also knew that calling Maureen would not be the end. Usually, after giving in to discouragement in one way, it just gets harder to avoid. So, empty television, "comfort" eating, social media ... and I just keep feeling worse. When I finally do pray—at least I did do it—I pray poorly and just to finish. The day ends badly, and often the next morning also begins badly. How do I understand times like this? Spiritually, what is going on? I think of myself as a spiritual person, a woman of prayer. Why, then, do evenings like this happen? How can I be drawn to such empty things?*

∞

Have you ever felt what Beth feels? Ever experienced times like these? Yes, of course; all of us have. In spiritual terms, how should we understand such times, and how should we respond to them?

Beth, after a difficult day, experiences nonspiritual desolation: she is tired physically and discouraged emotionally. Into this vulnerable space the enemy brings the further burden of spiritual desolation, and specifically what Ignatius calls a "movement to low and earthly things." Obviously, telephones, refrigerators, the Internet, and similar things serve in good ways: that is why we have them. But, like Beth, in time of spiritual desolation we may feel drawn to them in "low" and "earthly" ways—that is, in ways harmful to us spiritually.

That Beth—and we—feel this pull in time of spiritual desolation should not surprise us, nor is there any shame in feeling this pull. It is simply a tactic of the enemy, a form of spiritual desolation. Again, such is the spiritual life in a fallen but redeemed and loved world.

What does matter and matters greatly, is that we be discerning: that we note this pull to low and earthly things, identify it as the tactic of the enemy that it is, and, with God's grace and courage, reject it.

What if Beth, poised that evening between Evening Prayer and the phone call with Maureen, employs the tools Ignatius supplies for resisting spiritual desolation? What if she resolves not to make changes in time of desolation and, with courage, prays Evening Prayer at the usual time? What if she follows this with the examen prayer? Will she ever call Maureen that evening? Will the rest of the downward trajectory ever happen? And what if, to help her do this, she turns to prayer of petition, meditation, examination, and suitable penance, as described in the preceding chapter? What will her heart feel as she ends the day? As she rises the next morning?

Ignatius tells us that the pull toward low and earthly things is easiest to resist *in its very beginning* (rule 12). We know the truth of this: the longer we give in to this pull, the harder it is to resist. God's grace, however, is always with us, and resistance is always possible (see Phil. 4:13).

Elsewhere (rule 7), Ignatius invites the person in desolation to reflect that this is a *trial*; that is, this experience lies within God's loving providence and is permitted for reasons of love. When we resist spiritual desolation, we grow stronger spiritually. If Beth, in her apartment that evening, reflects on this, she will be strengthened to resist. And when the enemy, who is the liar, insinuates, "You're too weak. You'll give in to these low and earthly things. You always do. You'll pick up the phone. You'll let your prayer go. You can't stop yourself," Ignatius invites us to remember that *we can resist*, because of "the divine help that always remains" with us in time of desolation. Firmly rooted in the truth that *she can resist*, Beth is much more likely to resist in fact. The same is true for us.

Desolation, this lie of the enemy, is never the deepest reality in our spiritual lives. That is God's grace, felt less because of the desolation but always powerfully at work in us in time of desolation. I have always loved Ignatius's rules because of the hope they engender.

Lastly, we may note the enemy's insinuation in time of spiritual desolation that there is something wrong with us. The desolation—that is, the enemy—will say to us, "Look at you. Look at how you struggle. You are so poor in your spiritual life. There is something wrong with you." May I reverently ask, have you ever heard such voices? For most of us, perhaps all of us, the answer is yes. Obviously, if we believe this lie, it will burden us heavily.

When you experience spiritual desolation, the wonderful truth is that *there is nothing wrong with you.* Spiritual desolation in its various forms is simply a tactic of the enemy that every disciple of Jesus for two thousand years has experienced. To be aware of this tactic, to identify it for the lie that it is, and firmly to reject it sets us solidly on the path toward freedom.

7

"I'm Troubled, and I'm Tempted"

John sat in the office, waiting for the doctor to arrive. Before him was the doctor's chair and computer. Medical instruments surrounded him: cabinets with supplies, a rack with rubber gloves, another with paper towels, an instrument for monitoring blood pressure ... He watched the door nervously for the doctor's entrance.

The door opened. The doctor greeted John, sat, consulted the computer, and then turned to him. "The results of the biopsy are unclear," he said, "and I'm afraid that we'll need to do another." Seeing John's anxiety, the doctor added, "This does not necessarily mean anything bad. It just means that we didn't get the clarity we need. So, if you are okay with it, I'd like to do a second biopsy." Still uneasy, John agreed.

The doctor examined the growth on the right side of John's face. When all was prepared, he took the biopsy. "I'll be in touch in two weeks," he told John.

That evening, John shared the doctor's report with his wife, Jennie. He spoke calmly, but she sensed his worry. "John," she replied, "the doctor said it clearly. This is not bad news. It just means that he needs more clarity, and he is taking the proper steps to find it. Then we'll know what we're dealing with and how to proceed."

John smiled at her and replied, "You know me too well! Yes, you're right, and it helps to have you repeat the doctor's words. I'll try not to be too anxious."

∞

From John's journal, three days later:

> *"I'll try not to be too anxious": bold words, but hard to put into practice. I do worry, for myself, for Jennie if this should be serious, and for the children. I try to pray, to bring this to the Lord, and I give the time to prayer. But I'm restless. My thoughts are agitated and troubled. Today, I prayed Psalm 23, and that helped, at least for a time: "The Lord is my shepherd; there is nothing I lack." But then the churning starts again.*

From John's journal, two days later:

> *I continue to pray, to listen to the Bible app on my way to work, and to pray before retiring. But it's still unsettled. This evening, I hardly wanted to pray. Once again, I was uneasy and disturbed. I was alone in my study, and there was the phone. I know what happens when I'm feeling like this, and I go on the phone. I didn't do it, but I was very tempted.*

From John's journal, four days later:

> *Why doesn't prayer bring me peace? Why do I continue to feel agitated? I worry about the family, about my health, about what the doctor will say next week, about why I can't*

seem to overcome this churning even when I pray. The feeling is that others find peace through prayer—Jennie seems to—but that I can't. I wonder what's wrong with me. Am I missing something in the spiritual life? Doing something wrong? Why am I struggling like this? Why can't I feel God's closeness? And why, when I so need God and try to pray, do I feel these temptations to turn to the phone, the Internet, social media, even alcohol in ways that I know are harmful? And will I ever get through this? The feeling is that this will just go on . . .

Yes, why? The question is important. Is there any of us who has not felt, with his or her individual nuances, what John expresses here?

John experiences a form of spiritual desolation that Ignatius describes as "disquiet from various agitations and temptations." If John can identify his experience as the tactic of the enemy that it is—spiritual desolation—peace will begin to return, and he will be strengthened to resist it. If John is further aware that there is no shame in undergoing such spiritual desolation, that all do from time to time, he will be additionally encouraged in his struggle.

The enemy brings this spiritual desolation into a nonspiritual vulnerability in John: a place of worry—his understandable concern about the growth on his face and his anxiety as he awaits the results of the second biopsy. John deals well with this: he speaks with his wife, and he is faithful to prayer. Texts of the Bible help him. But even as he turns to the Lord, the enemy brings spiritual desolation, "disquiet from various agitations and temptations." This need not surprise John or us! Ignatius helps us understand this experience and points the way to freedom.

Struggles in the Spiritual Life

Disquiet: the opposite of peace, trouble of heart, restlessness. *From various agitations*: Why couldn't the doctor find clarity? What will the second biopsy show? What will happen to me and my family if my condition is serious? Why can't I find peace through my prayer? Why do I continue to be so unsettled? What I am I doing wrong in my spiritual life? Is there something wrong with me spiritually? Various agitations ... And *various temptations*: "Prayer is so hard this evening. Why don't you go on the phone for a while? Or on social media? Then you can pray. Or perhaps alcohol, and maybe a bit more of it, might help?" Or ... We can all supply the temptations the enemy brings us when we are agitated by spiritual desolation.

Ignatius alerts us to the fact that *temptations* (deceptive suggestions of the enemy) will mingle with *spiritual desolation* (heaviness of heart on the spiritual level). These are two ordinary, undramatic tactics of the enemy, and we all experience them. To be aware of them, name them, and reject them preserves us from spiritual harm.

John asks, "*I wonder what's wrong with me. Am I missing something in the spiritual life? Doing something wrong? Why am I struggling like this?*" His questions highlight another quality of spiritual desolation: the enemy's attempt to tell us that, if we experience it, this is because there *is something wrong with us*. No! Emphatically no! Spiritual desolation, as just said, is a common tactic of the enemy. We all experience it. There is no surprise that we do. To know this relieves a burden that God does not want us to carry and energizes us to reject the enemy's lies.

John also writes, "*And will I ever get through this? The feeling is that this will just go on.*" We will often feel this in time of desolation: the sense that this heaviness will go on and on, that the burden will persist, that the next day, the next week, even the next months and beyond, will be similarly desolate. May I reverently ask: Have you ever felt this? Ignatius urges the person in desolation to "think that he will soon be consoled" (rule 8). *Soon.* In time of spiritual desolation, he says, think, ponder, consider this truth: the present desolation will pass, consolation will return, and this will happen much sooner than the enemy—the liar and father of lies—would have you believe.

In time of desolation, never make a change (rule 5); resist the desolation with prayer of petition, meditation, examination, and suitable penance (rule 6); remember that God gives you all the grace you need to overcome the desolation (rule 7); and consider that, contrary to what the desolation would have you believe, consolation will return soon (rule 8). Ignatius continues to trace the path to freedom.

8

"I'm Going to Fail"

First e-mail from Julie to Emily:

*It's been a blessed day, and I'm so glad I came on this
retreat. When the pastor invited us to this weekend, I hesitated. I'd never been on a retreat before. But last night, when
I arrived and joined the others for supper, I immediately felt
at home. It's uplifting to be with good people who want to
grow spiritually.*

*You've mentioned Father Reed often, but this is the first
time I've met him and heard him speak. You can't help but
like him. He is low-key, but his words penetrate, and they
awaken desire for God. This evening's conference was on
holiness in the lay vocation, and it's made me think. And
not just think: it's made me want that.*

*After the talk, I went to the chapel. The Blessed Sacra-
ment was exposed on the altar, and I felt close to God. I also
felt happy in a way I've long wished for. I made two deci-
sions. Father invited us to consider praying Morning Prayer
and Evening Prayer from the Liturgy of the Hours. He
mentioned the shortened form available through a monthly*

publication or an app. I've already downloaded the app. It will take only a few minutes in the morning and the evening, and it's all laid out for me in the app. I'm even wondering if Bob might be willing to join me in this.

The other decision was about the Saturday-morning group for brunch. You've invited me several times, and I've always hesitated. If the invitation is still good, I'd like to come. I believe that the support of women who are friends and who also share the spiritual life would be a help. What do you think?

Second e-mail from Julie to Emily, three days later:

Thank you for your warm reply: you encourage me. I look forward to the brunch with the others. I'll be there on Saturday. Also, I've begun praying Morning Prayer and Evening Prayer most days, and I like it. It's new for me. I've never prayed the psalms before or the Liturgy of the Hours, but it's easy to follow on the app, and the explanations help. I feel like I'm growing spiritually. I'm still thinking of asking Bob if he'd like to join me for Morning or Evening Prayer.

Third e-mail from Julie to Emily, ten days later:

When we spoke after brunch on Saturday, I told you how much I enjoyed it. I've always had friends, but it's different when you can talk about spiritual things. It really strengthens me. I suspect that this brunch may become an important part of my week. I can't thank you enough. Do you know, I think that the greater peace I feel since the retreat is helping the family too. Somehow, there seems to be more peace among us as well.

Fourth e-mail from Julie to Emily, a week later:

You asked if I'd spoken to Bob about Morning or Evening Prayer. I don't know if I will. We had a tense discussion last evening. Bob thinks I'm not helping our youngest son David in the way he needs, especially with his struggles at school. I'm doing the best I can to help him, and so this hits a vulnerable place in me. When that place is hit, something in me loses heart and withdraws. Bob always knows when I get like this, and it frustrates him because, from his perspective, he's just trying to improve things. It also bothers him when he sees that he has caused me pain, and so it gets complicated. Bob and I will talk about David again, but I don't know where it will go.

Fifth e-mail from Julie to Emily, ten days later:

I'm sorry that I missed the brunch on Saturday. I won't make excuses. I could have come as far as time goes. But I'm still discouraged about the conversation with Bob. It's not resolved yet. It affects my prayer too. I haven't been faithful to Morning Prayer and Evening Prayer, and when I do pray them, they don't have the same life. I'm beginning to wonder if that spiritual "growth" from the retreat was as real as I thought. It doesn't seem to take much to undo it.

Sixth e-mail from Julie to Emily, five days later:

I know it would have been good to be there on Saturday, but I felt that I just couldn't do it. I've been a Catholic all my life, and my faith is important to me. But I've never been as

committed as you and, from what I see, the other women at
the brunch. I thought that the retreat had changed that, and
you know that I've been trying since then. But here I am, in
the same place again, going back on the resolutions I made
at the retreat. Maybe I'm just not meant for a deep prayer
life. Maybe the way I've lived my faith until now is the way
it will be.

Seventh e-mail from Julie to Emily, two weeks later:

I appreciate your encouragement. You know that it means
a lot to me. If I live my faith as much as I do, part of it
is because of you, and I'm grateful. But I think you see a
potential in me that isn't there. If it were, why I have I lived
the spiritual life so superficially all these years? And why,
when I try to grow, do I always wind up back at the same
place? I'm up, then so quickly down. You and the others
seem so much more stable and so faithful. I must be different. I'm not happy about it, but there it is.

Eighth e-mail from Julie to Emily, one week later:

I find myself thinking like this: You believed you were growing in love of God. Look at you now. You're not faithful
to prayer, you don't get along with your husband, and you
don't take good care of your son. You've been fooling yourself. You thought that the retreat was a time of grace, and
you thought that God was calling you to grow spiritually.
Look at how poorly it's all going. How do you know that
was God? How do you know you heard his voice? To judge
by the results, you didn't.

Here's another question. I have all the failings that
I've mentioned, but we say that God loves us. Well, I was
doing my best to grow closer to God, to love God, and to live
my vocation more fully. Then this happens, and it all falls
apart. Couldn't a God who loves me spare me this? Why
does he let this happen to people who try to love him?

Much to sift through spiritually! First, what is Julie experiencing at this point? After a blessed retreat and time of spiritual energy, a tense conversation with her husband touches a vulnerable place. Julie experiences nonspiritual desolation, that is, emotional heaviness, self-doubt, and discouragement. As already seen, the enemy works in emotionally vulnerable places. Here he brings a form of spiritual desolation that Ignatius describes as "lack of confidence."

Those who, like Julie, experience this kind of spiritual desolation—no shame!—find themselves doubting, questioning, revisiting things that had seemed so clear, and all of this with trouble of heart, with a sense that, "I can't," "It will never work out," "I'll fail again," "Others can pray and grow in holiness, but not I," and the like.

Thus, Julie: "*You thought you were growing in love of God.... You've been fooling yourself. You thought that the retreat was a time of grace, and you thought that God was calling you to grow spiritually... How do you know that was God? How do you know you heard his voice?*" And again, "*Maybe I'm just not meant for a deep prayer life. Maybe the way I've lived my faith until now is the way it will be.*" Julie experiences the "lack of confidence" that Ignatius identifies as spiritual desolation. Have you ever felt something similar?

The "beauty" of this, to use an odd word in this context, is that *all of this is a lie.* Julie *is* growing in love of God: the tense conversation with Bob that these two, who love each other, will resolve in their own way and time, does not change this. Julie is *not* fooling herself. The retreat *was* a time of grace. God *did* invite her to take new spiritual steps. Julie *is* meant—as God's grace during the retreat and afterward shows—to deepen her life of prayer. If Julie is aware of the enemy's tactic, identifies it as such, and rejects it, her present spiritual growth will continue.

Reread Julie's seventh and eighth e-mails (first paragraph). When you experience a similar lack of confidence, recognize these thoughts for the lies that they are. Reject them! Continue without faltering on your spiritual path. God *is* calling you to grow! And with His grace, with His love that always accompanies you, that growth is possible.

Julie's experience permits an important observation. If the enemy ordinarily brings *spiritual* desolation into areas of *nonspiritual* vulnerability (tiredness, discouragement, depression, and the like), then whatever you do to reduce or eliminate that nonspiritual vulnerability will greatly ease your spiritual life. If, for example, Julie and Bob communicate and resolve their tension, Julie will find herself much less susceptible to the "lack of confidence" described here. The same is true for all of us when we experience nonspiritual vulnerabilities.

Julie also writes, "*I'm up, then so quickly down. You and the others seem so much more stable and so faithful. I must be different.*" A further lie of desolation is this: "It's just you. Other people don't go through this. You're up, then down. Other people are steady. *It's only you.*" Again, emphatically no! When Julie knows the others better, and they share on a deeper level, she will find that *all* undergo these ups (times of spiritual energy, of feeling God's closeness—that is, of spiritual consolation) and downs (times without spiritual energy, of not feeling God's closeness—that is, of spiritual desolation). If you experience times of spiritual consolation and times of spiritual desolation, then you share the experience of every man or woman who has ever loved the Lord. What matters is—by now you can tell me!—to be aware, understand, and take action. Take action: that is, to accept God's gift of spiritual consolation and to reject the enemy's discouraging lies in spiritual desolation.

In her last e-mail, Julie raises a key question: "*I was doing my best to grow closer to God, to love God, and to live my vocation more fully. Then this happens, and it all falls apart. Couldn't a God who loves me spare me this? Why does he let this happen to people who try to love him?*" Yes, why? Who of us has not asked this at some point?

Ignatius understands the importance of this question and reverences it. He dedicates to it one of his lengthiest rules (rule 9). His answer is: if we go through times of spiritual desolation in the way described—that is, aware of it, able to name it, and striving to reject it—then not only does the desolation not harm us but we grow spiritually in rich ways. At times, the desolation helps us see areas of regression and address them; at other times, God permits desolation because we learn and grow stronger spiritually through the struggle; finally, God may permit desolation to keep us from complacency in the spiritual life, to help us remain "poor in spirit" (Matt. 5:3) and so ready to receive his grace.[13] If Julie and we know this, we will be greatly strengthened in the struggle against desolation.

---

[13] God does not *give* spiritual desolation; this is always a work of the enemy. God may *permit* the enemy to visit us with spiritual desolation for reasons of love—because of the growth that follows when we resist it, as Ignatius indicates in rule 9. See Gallagher, *The Discernment of Spirits*, 67.

9

"I'll Try, but Nothing Will Come of It"

The phone rang in the parish office. Moments later, the call was transferred to Father Reed's desk. He answered and said, "Hello, this is Father Reed." His caller replied, "Good morning, Father. My name is Bob Johnson. You don't know me, but my wife, Julie, made the retreat you gave three months ago. She loved the retreat and spoke well of you. I'm struggling with some things in my spiritual life, and I wondered if you'd be willing to meet with me." They made an appointment for Saturday at one o'clock.

Saturday arrived, and they sat in the rectory parlor. After their initial exchanges and a brief prayer, Father Reed settled himself to listen.

Bob began, "Maybe it's best that I give a little background about the things I want to talk about."

Father Reed nodded his agreement.

"I've been a Catholic all my life, and I go to Mass every Sunday with Julie and the children. Julie and I have been married for seventeen years. We've had our ups and downs, but I've always thought of it as a good marriage. Still, every so often I hurt Julie. I don't mean to, and I realize it only after it's happened. I see her withdraw, and I know she's suffering. I did it again a few weeks ago when—with what I thought were good intentions—I raised questions about how she's working with our youngest son, David, who is struggling at school. It really bothers me when I do this, and I try to make amends. It can get complicated. Usually, after some days, we resolve the tension. This time, though, it's still there."

Father Reed nodded once more and continued to listen.

"Spiritually, things have been moving in a good direction over these last years. I've joined the Men's Faith Formation Group in the parish, and we meet on first and third Fridays in the morning. It's been good in many ways. I've made some good friends, I've learned more about prayer, and my faith seems more alive. That's why it's so discouraging when this tension with Julie happens again, and I recognize that I'm not treating her in the way she needs. It starts to affect everything: my relationship with her and the children, my work, even my prayer. That's why I'm here. I need help."

"How does the discouragement affect you, Bob?" asked Father Reed.

"I find myself thinking like this: 'What kind of a husband are you? You hear talks about how married men grow in holiness by loving their wives and children. You want to be that kind of man. But look at the mess you make of your relationship with your wife. Don't think you'll ever be much of husband and not much of a father either. You can't even agree with your wife about how to help your son. Make all the efforts you want. Maybe you'll do better in this or that for a while. But you'll never really change.'"

"That sounds pretty heavy," Father Reed said.

"It is, and it doesn't stop there. As I said, it spreads to everything."

"Could you say more about that, Bob? What's that like?"

"Well, for example, I mentioned the Men's Faith Formation Group. Friday morning comes, and I find myself thinking, 'What's the point of going? You've been attending these meetings for two years, and where has it gotten you? Nothing has changed. Why bother going?' To be honest, recently I have missed some of the meetings.

"One of the recommendations is to spend a few minutes daily with the readings from the day's Mass. I subscribe to a monthly publication with the readings, and I pray with them in the evening. And the same thought comes: 'Why bother? What good has it done? Go ahead, pray with the readings, but it won't make any difference. You won't change.' Sometimes, I give in and just don't do it."

"That does sound difficult," Father Reed agreed.

"I'll add one more thing," Bob continued, "and then I'll have said all I need to say. I've been wondering about making a retreat. Julie made one, and I saw how it helped her. That got me thinking about doing the same. I know you'll be doing another retreat two months from now, and I've considered signing up. But there it is: 'What's the point? Sign up, go, be a part of it. You'll hear some good things, and you may make some good resolutions. It might even change things for a few weeks. But it won't last. You'll go back to being the same you. You'll hurt your wife again, you'll disappoint your children, you'll pull out of the group, you'll drop your prayer—just like you're doing now.' So, I haven't registered for the retreat." Bob stopped speaking and looked at Father Reed.

Father Reed was silent for a moment. Then he said, "Bob, I appreciate your honesty. I imagine that it was not easy to say the things you have. I'm so glad that you've been able to put that into words. Let me ask: As you hear yourself say all this, does anything strike you?"

"What do you mean, Father?" Bob asked.

"Well, you've spoken of your relationship with Julie, with your son David, your participation in the men's group, your evening prayer, and the retreat. What do you see happening in these different areas?"

Now Bob was silent. Father Reed gave him the time he needed.

"I think," Bob said slowly, "that there is something common to them all."

"Can you say what it is?"

"Yes, I think so. The areas are different, but the thought is the same for each: make your efforts if you want, but nothing will really change. These efforts won't last. You'll always be the same mediocre — or worse — husband, father, member of the group, person of prayer that you are now."

Father Reed nodded his agreement. "It's good that you can see that," he said. "What happens when you believe that thought?"

"What happens is what *is* happening: I lose hope. I give up hope of not hurting Julie, of ever being a better father. I stop going to the meetings on Fridays. I don't pray in the evening. I decide not to make the retreat."

"Yes, that's what happens when you believe that thought. Bob, let me ask this: Do you love Julie?"

"Of course I do."

"Do you think she knows that?"

"Yes, I know she does."

"You said earlier that there are tensions from time to time, but you've always thought of your marriage as a good one. Do you continue to think that's true?"

"Yes, I don't doubt it."

"Do you think Julie would say the same?"

"Yes, I'm sure she would."

"Do you love your children? Do you want the best for David?"

"Yes, absolutely."

"Are your children happy?"

"They have struggles, as we all do in growing up, but, yes, I think they are happy."

"Bob," Father Reed asked, "how does all that you've just said—and said with such sincerity and confidence—compare with the thought you've described, that you're not a good husband, not a good father, that you never will be, that you'll never be holy in this vocation, that there's no point in going to the men's group, in praying in the evening, or in making a retreat?"

For the first time, Bob smiled. "Well, when you put it like that," he said, "it sounds like I've been giving these thoughts too much power. It sounds like they don't correspond to reality and that things are not as dark as I've believed."

"Yes, I'd say that's right. Bob, let me ask you this: When you believe these thoughts, what happens?"

"That's simple. I give up. I stop trying because there's no point: nothing will change."

Father Reed nodded. "Bob, there is a tempter who wants to discourage you, especially when both you and Julie are growing spiritually in such a wonderful way. It's not surprising that you find these thoughts—these lies—presenting themselves, and there's no shame in experiencing them. What matters is to identify them for the lies that they are, reject them, and stay firmly on track toward God.

"I say 'these lies' because everything you say shows that you are a man of faith, that you love God, that you pray, that you want to grow spiritually, that you love your wife and your children, that you are a good husband and father and want to grow in this calling. This is who you are. Yes, certainly, like me, like all of us, you can grow and need to grow. But that does not change your identity. Reject the lies. Pray faithfully. Find ways to let Julie know that you love her, and do the same with your son. Just stay on track, Bob, and you'll see that things will work out well."

Bob looked at Father Reed. He was deeply moved. "I can't tell you how grateful I am," he said, "It's like waking from a bad dream."

∽

With Father Reed's help, Bob recognizes a tactic of the enemy, another form of spiritual desolation. Ignatius describes this as "lack of hope." When we experience this form of desolation, our thoughts are like Bob's: we lose hope of any real progress in loving God, in prayer, in holiness, and in living our vocation well. If we think like this, we will be tempted, like Bob, to give up—precisely the enemy's goal.

All of this is a lie! If ever you feel "defeated before you begin" in your spiritual life, recognize the lie of the enemy and reject it. Do not relinquish your efforts to grow spiritually. God's love and the power of his grace are with you in these efforts. Compared with this, the enemy's lies are a very small thing.

Further, we can prepare to reject such lies *even before the enemy brings them* (Ignatius's rule 10). After this attack by the enemy, for example, Bob can prepare himself to reject similar lies should the enemy bring them again.

Let us suppose that Bob, restored in peace, sits in his study or before the Blessed Sacrament, or in conversation with Julie, and reviews the experience of the past weeks. He notes, or he and Julie together note, the enemy's discouraging lies and the vulnerability (their tension after speaking about David) that exposed him to them. Bob plans how he will resist these lies when, as is likely—again, no shame!—they return: how he will not change his prayer, will not distance himself from the men's group, will talk with Julie and seek her help, will perhaps meet with Father Reed, and the like. Bob and Julie resolve that if either experiences these lies, he or she will tell the other for mutual support in the struggle.

If they do this, they will be greatly strengthened to resist quickly and decisively when the enemy's "lack of hope" presents itself again.

How might you be vulnerable to this lack of hope in your spiritual life? Can you prepare ahead, prepare even now? If you do, like Bob and Julie, you will find future desolation easier to overcome.

A final comment, and one of great importance: the enemy will try to convince you that what you experience in spiritual desolation is your identity: it is *who you are spiritually*. Do you feel far from God this evening (spiritual desolation)? This is *who you are*: a person far from God (spiritual identity). Do you feel little desire to pray today (spiritual desolation)? This is *who you are*: a person who does not love prayer (spiritual identity). Do you feel little energy today to attend daily Mass as usual (spiritual desolation)? This is *who you are*: a person who does not love the Eucharist (spiritual identity).

No! And again no! You are a person close to God, who loves prayer and who loves the Eucharist—this is why you have these practices!—but whom God, for reasons of a love we have already seen (chapter 8), is permitting to experience spiritual desolation. Reject the enemy's false equation between the spiritual desolation you experience and your spiritual identity. When you do, your struggles will lighten and your spiritual energy will increase.

10

"I Don't Feel God's Love"

From Cathy's journal, Wednesday evening:

I've never kept a journal before, but I'm willing to try. Father Bauer suggested that we do this during these six weeks of prayer. I hopeful that these weeks will teach me how to pray with Scripture. I've never known how to do that, and I've always wanted to learn. This evening we had our first meeting in the parish. There were sixty people there. Father Bauer gave us a talk on how to pray with the Bible. I found it interesting, and the way he explained it, it seems like something I can do. After he finished, we talked about it in small groups. I enjoyed that too. Then Father gave us the Scriptures to pray with until we meet next week. We'll be doing this for six weeks.

Father asked us to give fifteen or twenty minutes to this daily if we can. That seems possible. He also suggested keeping a daily journal and noting briefly at the end of the prayer how it went. He proposed two questions for this review: What was I thinking? What was I feeling?

It's all new to me, and I find it engaging. I look forward to starting tomorrow.

Struggles in the Spiritual Life

From Cathy's journal, Thursday morning of week one:

> *Today's passage was on Bartimaeus (Mark 10:46–52). I
> had no trouble praying with it for twenty minutes. It makes
> a nice start to the day, like being fed spiritually. As I began,
> I took a moment, the way Father said, to see Jesus's look of
> love upon me. Then I read the passage slowly and saw myself
> there, in the scene. For a time, I just repeated Bartimaeus's
> prayer, "Jesus, Son of David, have pity on me." As I did,
> peace entered my heart. I felt that Jesus was near, that he
> heard my prayer, and that he would help me and heal me, as
> he did Bartimaeus.*

From Cathy's journal, Monday morning of week two:

> *This is the fifth day, and it continues to go well. Today's
> passage is Isaiah 43:1–7. "You are precious in my eyes and
> honored, and I love you" (v. 4). This message speaks to my
> heart and to a place that can feel too alone and afraid. The
> time passed quickly. I go now to the day with a sense of be-
> ing loved and of God's closeness.*

From Cathy's journal, Friday morning of week two:

> *I begin to understand why people pray daily with Scripture.
> God's word is really starting to feel like God's word to me,
> not just a book to revere, but a word spoken by a Person to
> me. Today's passage is Psalm 139:1–18. "Behind and before
> you encircle me and rest your hand upon me.... You knit me
> in my mother's womb. I praise you, because I am wonder-
> fully made.... My very self you know" (vv. 5, 13–14). I've*

never realized that God is this close to me, that he shaped
me so personally and so lovingly. I find that I want to praise
him. Again, this morning, I go to the day feeling loved and
accompanied.

From Cathy's journal, Thursday morning of week three:

> Last night, Father Bauer explained that we can pray a
> Gospel passage by living it from within, being there, and tak-
> ing part. I did that with this morning's passage, Zacchaeus's
> encounter with Jesus (Luke 19:1–10). I know that feeling of
> being on the outside, less than others, poorer than others in
> my relationship with God. Somehow, I was there in the tree,
> waiting for Jesus. I delighted in seeing him set aside every-
> thing just to be with me. I felt like he and I were together
> the way he and Zacchaeus were in Zacchaeus's house. I also
> felt that, like Zacchaeus, something was changing in me. As
> these weeks pass, I'm beginning to sense something new in
> my relationship with Jesus. The best way I can say it is that
> he is becoming real for me in a new way. I'm also finding
> it easier to reach out to others, to listen, to offer help, to be
> patient. I don't want this to end when the six weeks finish.

From Cathy's journal, Saturday morning of week four:

> Today I prayed with Jesus's encounter with the Samaritan
> woman (John 4:1–42). Maybe it was because I was tired,
> because this passage was much longer than the others, or
> because there are things in John's Gospel that I don't under-
> stand, but I had a harder time getting into it this morning.
> That was a disappointment because I was looking forward

to praying with this passage. Father Bauer spoke beautifully
of it on Wednesday. I did my best, but nothing really struck
me. Father told us to expect days like this, and I understand
that this is part of any daily life of prayer. It's probably a
good thing that I experience it during these six weeks of
learning.

From Cathy's journal, Friday morning of week five:

We prayed with Matthew 8:23–27, the calming of the
storm. I settled in as usual to pray. I was there in the boat
with the disciples and Jesus, who slept while the storm arose.
But when I heard him ask, "Why are you terrified, O you
of little faith?" everything changed. "Why are you terrified?"
Why?? Because there is a storm raging, we are in danger of
death, and you are sleeping!

Suddenly, I was back ten years, when I had the cancer
that meant I'd never have children. I was afraid then, too,
and you slept. I grew angry in this prayer in a way I never
have before. Why were you terrified? Didn't I have reason to
be terrified? Why did you sleep? That's the real question.

From Cathy's journal, Saturday morning of week five:

Yesterday's prayer and questions are still churning in me.
Today's passage was the multiplication of the loaves and
fish (Matt. 14:13–21). It's all about Jesus's compassion for
the crowd, His healings, and His concern for their hunger.
None of this spoke to me. As I sit here in my room, I don't
feel His compassion. I don't feel His closeness. I don't feel
His love. He seems distant, like I'm here and He is far

*away. I don't rise from this prayer feeling ready to be patient
and compassionate toward others. Why should I pray on
days like today? I almost feel worse for having prayed with
this passage.*

From Cathy's journal, Sunday morning of week six:

*The Scripture for prayer was the resurrection of Lazarus
(John 11:1–44). When Jesus hears that Lazarus is deathly
ill, when his sisters plead with Jesus to come and remind
him of his love for Lazarus, "he remained for two days in
the place where he was." And Lazarus dies. Once more, that
place of pain and anger was touched in me. Again, today,
I don't feel God's love or compassion. All that warmth I
felt in the first weeks – "You are precious.... I love you....
Behind and before you encircle me and rest your hand upon
me" – all of that is gone. I wonder if it was even real. I don't
feel loved. I feel abandoned. I feel alone. I hurt. I can't go
on like this. I want to quit praying. Why should I pray when
this happens? I need to speak with someone who can help me
make sense out of this.*

∞

We have reached a deep place in Cathy's relationship with the
Lord, and we must approach it with great reverence and sensitivity.
She asks important questions. What happened when she prayed
with the words, "Why are you terrified?" Why did things change?
What is she experiencing now? How should she respond to this?
Was the warmth of the first weeks real? Yes, conversation with a
competent spiritual director would help.

In her first weeks of prayer, Cathy experiences rich spiritual consolation. Prayer is alive, God feels close, and his love is real for her. Cathy delights in this newness, and she feels herself more ready to love others. In weeks five and six, this changes. Now Cathy experiences spiritual desolation. She finds herself, to use Ignatius's words, "without love." She does not feel God's love. All the earlier warmth is gone. And, as she also writes, "*I don't rise from this prayer feeling ready to be patient and compassionate toward others.*"

This is yet another form of spiritual desolation: times when we feel no sense of God's love, of His closeness, of warm love for others in God, but rather, we feel a kind of spiritual distance and coldness. As we've said so often, there is no shame in experiencing this. To feel this form of spiritual desolation does *not* mean that God does not love us, that we do not love Him, or that we do not desire to love others. It simply means that God is permitting us to undergo a time of spiritual desolation because of the growth we gain when we go through it well (see the final paragraph of chapter 8).

Cathy's spiritual desolation as she prays with the calming of the storm is actually a sign that her prayer is progressing richly. For ten years, a wound in her heart has remained unhealed. God loves her too much to allow this to continue unaddressed. Almost inevitably, as she grows closer to God in prayer, this wound is touched. When it is, spiritual desolation results: pain, anger, a sense of distance from God, and an absence of all warmth. If Cathy finds wise counsel to help her understand this and if she does not stop praying, then, for the first time in ten years, deep spiritual healing can occur. Like the disciples in the boat and like Lazarus's sisters, she will find that if Jesus slept and if he delayed two days, it was because he loved them and had a greater gift to give.

∞

Cathy experiences, as we do, both spiritual consolation (uplifting movements of the heart on the spiritual level) and spiritual desolation (heavy movements of the heart on the spiritual level). This is normal in the spiritual life, and God's loving providence includes both. In times of spiritual consolation, God pours love, grace, energy, and creativity into our spiritual journey. When he permits the enemy to bring spiritual desolation, God does so because, through resisting it, we grow in other key ways.

We need, therefore, Ignatius tells us, to remain humble—not naively high, thinking that all struggles are past—in time of spiritual consolation; and we need to remain trusting—not despairingly low, thinking that all is lost—in time of spiritual desolation (rule 11). Joyfully humble in consolation and confidently trusting in desolation: this is the path to spiritual progress.

In times of spiritual desolation, we may feel a sense of irreparable disaster: "It's over! You've failed. It's all going badly. It won't change. The darkness you experience, the heaviness of heart, the pull to low and earthly things, the loss of hope, is a disaster, and it is irreparable." Again, and with great emphasis, no! Yes, the desolation is difficult. But as we have seen, it is an experience that God permits out of love and one that offers blessed opportunities of growth.

11

"I Don't Have the Energy"

Supper was over, and the house was quiet. Bob turned to Julie and suggested that they go for a walk. This had become a practice that both welcomed. Ten minutes later, they left the house and began their usual circuit of the neighborhood. The summer sun lit the rows of houses, the trees, and the parked cars.

As they walked, they spoke of the day's happenings, of the children, and of their work. It was good to be together and to share.

The conversation turned to Bob's role in the Men's Faith Formation Group. Two years earlier, the leader had moved, and the pastor had asked Bob to take his place. Both Bob and Julie had thought it a good idea, and Bob accepted. He enjoyed the task and found that it helped him spiritually. Under his leadership, the group flourished, nearly doubling in size.

Julie asked Bob how he was finding it now. She was not surprised when Bob did not answer immediately.

"It's been good," he said slowly, "and you know how I've enjoyed it these past two years. I think God is more at the center of my life because of it, and I feel closer to the Church. We both know, too, that good things have happened for our marriage and the family."

Julie nodded and said, "But something has been different recently, hasn't it?"

"Yes, it has. How did you know?"

"I know you, and I know when something is troubling you."

"Well, you're right. It has been different these last few months and maybe longer than that."

"Different in what way? Do you mind talking about it?"

"You know, I both do and don't. I do, because I need to talk about it, and I know you'll understand. I don't, because it's embarrassing, and it's not easy for me to talk about things like this." Julie continued to walk beside him.

"Maybe it started," Bob said, "when I realized that few of the men ever said thank you for the work I was doing. One of them also complained about the format of the meetings on Fridays. I didn't show it, but inside I was saying, 'Can't you appreciate what others do for you? Can't you do anything but complain? If you don't like it, don't come. We'll manage without you.' Maybe this has nothing to do with what I'm feeling. I don't know."

They turned a corner onto another street.

"What I do know," Bob said, "is that prayer has been difficult recently. It's felt dry and empty. I don't feel nourished by it, and to be honest, I don't really want to do it. I have to force myself to pray, and sometimes I don't. I don't know what's going on. I'm still praying the same way, but I don't seem to have energy for it."

Bob looked at Julie. "And I feel the same about the group," he continued. "No one would say that I'm lazy, and I don't believe that I am, but that's the feeling. I just don't want to make the effort to search for another speaker, make sure he's right for the group, get the pastor's approval, contact the speaker, make the arrangements, make sure the parish hall is ready, and all the rest of it."

Julie listened silently as Bob spoke.

"I guess what I'm saying," Bob continued, "is that I'm tired of it. It's not a physical tiredness. It's just a lack of desire, a lack of the enthusiasm I used to feel. What troubles me, too, is that I feel this way about almost everything in my spiritual life. That's what you've noticed, haven't you?"

"Yes," Julie answered, "and I'd been hoping you talk about it. I'm glad that you are now."

"This is the feeling: I don't have energy for spiritual things. I have to make myself do them. Those new steps I've been taking to grow as a husband and father—that desire is gone too. At least, I don't feel it. And, as I'm saying, it's also true of the group. You know, Julie, I think it may be time for me to stop leading the group. Maybe the way I feel says that I've given what I can. I've been doing it for two years. Maybe the group needs someone new. I've been thinking of saying this to Father."

"I'm not surprised," Julie replied. "I imagined that your thoughts must be turning that way."

"Well, what do you think?"

It was Julie's turn not to answer immediately. They walked in silence for a minute. Then Julie said, "I think that something is not right about this. You're doing excellent work with the group. More men than ever come, and it continues to grow. Maybe they haven't said it, but that certainly is a thank-you—and one more powerful than words. If you step down, I think it will hurt the group.

"And another thing strikes me as well. This lack of energy you describe is not limited to your part in the group. It seems to touch everything in your spiritual life: your prayer, your role as husband, as father, the newness you've been seeking—everything. That makes me wonder if the issue is not the group and the other things. Maybe this lack of energy is about something different."

Bob looked at Julie. "If it is about something different, what would that be?"

"I don't know," she said, "but you can't be the first person to experience this in the spiritual life. I'm sure we can find answers. And I don't think you should decide about stepping down until we have answers."

"I think you're right," Bob said. "The longer this goes on, the heavier it gets. It is time to find answers."

∞

Julie is right. Bob is not the first one to experience this lack of spiritual energy. Is there any of us who has not felt this at times? You love the spiritual life, you live it willingly and joyfully, but ... now your energy is diminished. It may even feel totally absent. You have almost to make yourself pray as usual, almost to make yourself attend that Bible study you have so loved, almost to make yourself pursue that spiritual growth you so desired.

When Bob feels this, when we feel this, we are experiencing a form of spiritual desolation that Ignatius describes as "finding oneself totally slothful."

In this form of desolation, we feel spiritually sluggish, indolent, lazy, lackadaisical. The adverb "totally" is powerful: in time of spiritual desolation, we may feel *totally* sluggish, lazy, and slothful as regards various aspects of our spiritual lives. We feel no energy for prayer, for God's service, for involvement in our parish, for holiness in our vocations, and the like. The feeling of slothfulness in spiritual desolation may contrast sharply with the energy we more habitually feel for these same things when not in desolation.

There is no shame in experiencing this form of spiritual desolation. We all do at times. What is important—Julie is on target with this—is to be aware of it, understand it for the tactic of the enemy that it is, and firmly reject it. For Bob, this means that he should not renounce leadership of the group until he has greater clarity about his spiritual situation (rule 5: in time of desolation, never make a change). That change will not resolve his lack of energy; identifying and rejecting the desolation will. Bob may further apply the means Ignatius offers to resist and overcome the desolation: prayer of petition, meditation, examination, suitable penance, and the rest.

Bob adds, *"The longer this goes on, the heavier it gets."* Yes: if we do not resist spiritual desolation, the longer it goes on, the heavier it will get. The contrary is also true: the sooner we identify and resist the enemy's desolations (for Bob, feeling totally slothful in the spiritual life) and associated temptations (for Bob, to renounce leadership of the group, with consequent harm to himself and the group), the easier it is to reject them. What if Bob had applied Ignatius's counsels two months earlier, and had identified and rejected his spiritual desolation at that time? Most likely, those two months would have been very different. The slothful feeling would have diminished or disappeared entirely, and the temptation to renounce the leadership would likewise have weakened or ceased altogether.

Ignatius makes this point in his rule 12: identify and resist the enemy's temptations and desolations as soon as you can. To apply a metaphor, stop the snowball *at the top of the mountain* before it can gain mass and speed. The further down the mountainside it advances, the harder it will be to stop it. If we resist in the very beginning or as close to it as we can, our task will be greatly lightened.

Saint Benedict writes, "As soon as wrongful thoughts come into your heart, dash them against Christ"[14]—*as soon as.* Likewise,

---

[14] Gallagher, *Setting Captives Free: Personal Reflections on Ignatian Discernment of Spirits* (New York: Crossroad, 2018), 213.

Saint Augustine: "Something contrary to God's law comes into your mind. Do not keep your mind on this, do not consent to it. What comes into your mind is the head of the serpent. Crush the head and you will avoid the rest of the movement. What does it mean to crush the head of the serpent? To reject that suggestion."[15] And in *The Imitation of Christ* we read, "We must watch, therefore, above all for the beginning of temptation, because then the enemy is more easily overcome."[16]

Associated with this is another quality of spiritual desolation that I call "pre-event desolation." You are about to begin prayer. You will leave in four days for a weekend retreat. This evening, you will offer reflections for a parish group. The program of spiritual formation will begin next week. Tomorrow, you will meet with a spiritual director. And so forth. In these and similar situations, as the time draws near, you experience a lack of desire, a discouragement. Thoughts like these arise: "Why bother? It won't change anything. You'll get there and find it hard. You never should have signed up for that. Why put yourself through it? Another time, a different setting will be better. Let it go. Why don't you call and cancel?"

Of course the enemy does not want you to pray, to make that retreat, to speak with that person, and the like! Watch for this pre-prayer, pre-retreat, pre–parish group, pre-conversation desolation. Do not let it stop you, and these steps will bless your spiritual life.

---

[15] St. Augustine, on Psalm 103, 4th sermon.
[16] Gallagher, *Setting Captives Free*, 213.

12

"I Have No Fervor"

Beth opened the door and entered her apartment. It was 5:30 p.m. on Wednesday, and she had just returned from work. It was time to begin her Wednesday evening routine—and she had no desire to do it.

Three years earlier, Beth had begun the diocesan Bible school, a four-year program of formation in the Bible. She came to love the program. For the first time in her life, she understood the Bible. The classes were interesting and the group discussions engaging. Beth made new friends through the program. Above all, her relationship with God had changed, had grown, had deepened. Knowing more deeply that she was loved, Beth grew less anxious and found more energy for life. Now, when she heard the readings at Mass, she knew their context. They spoke to her, and they nourished her. Currently, they were discussing the prophets, and tonight they would begin Hosea.

Beth changed and prepared supper. Perhaps it was tiredness from a full day; perhaps it was discouragement from tension with Susan; perhaps it was a need to relax and not have to face the next activity; perhaps it was … Beth did not know what it was. What she did know was that she had no desire to attend the Bible class. But she had made a commitment, and she would be faithful.

Beth made herself eat supper as usual. She made herself gather her books and materials. She made herself walk to the car, drive to the church, park the car, and enter the parish hall. She made herself smile and greet the others. Then she took her place. Shortly after, the teacher entered.

Beth did her best, but this evening the teaching did not appeal to her. It felt barren, empty, tasteless. The teacher spoke of the love language in Hosea, of the spousal imagery, of the God who draws his people "with bands of love" (Hos. 11:4). None of this resonated with Beth. None of it touched her heart. Nothing in her responded. She looked at her watch: forty-five minutes of lecture remained, and group discussion would follow. Beth only wanted it to end so she could return home.

She did her best, and she did it well. None could have guessed how little she wished to be there. Finally, it was over, and the last goodbye said. Beth left the hall and drove home.

As she did, thoughts churned within. What was wrong? What had changed? She had loved the Bible school through the earlier years. She knew that it had blessed her. Why was it so different now? Had she gained from it all she could? Was she at fault somehow? Beth had no answers. These questions weighed on her and discouraged her. She parked and entered her apartment. She foresaw a difficult evening. She also decided that she would speak once more with Father Reed.

∞

How should we understand Beth's experience this Wednesday evening? We have no indication that Beth is at fault. She is faithful. She prepares and attends the class in her usual way. She does her best to participate—so well in fact, that none perceive her lack of enthusiasm. What, then, is Beth experiencing?

Having followed Ignatius thus far, we can guess the answer! This Wednesday evening, Beth experiences a form of spiritual desolation. She feels, to use Ignatius's words, "totally tepid," that is, completely without fervor as she performs a spiritual practice.

In this form of desolation, we feel spiritually lukewarm, indifferent, unenthusiastic, without affect. When we pray, serve the Lord, live our vocations, take new steps in our spiritual lives, seek holiness, but find ourselves tepid and without fervor as we do these things, we are experiencing spiritual desolation. The adverb "totally" is again expressive.

Have you ever felt this form of spiritual desolation? Yes, certainly, we all have at times. Obviously, the enemy's goal is that such tepidity cause us to question ourselves, to lose heart, to abandon these helpful practices. Beth responds well when she remains faithful, the right response for us as well.

Once again, no shame! No surprise! Be aware, identify, reject.

Beth wisely decides to speak with Father Reed. In doing so, she applies another Ignatian guideline (rule 13): in times of burden, temptation, and desolation, do not face these alone; find a wise and competent spiritual person—a spiritual director, mentor, priest, religious, spouse, or friend—and *speak about the burden*. Throughout this book, we have seen people do so and always with blessed results.

Is there spiritual heaviness in your heart? Are you discouraged? Are you afraid? Have you suffered this for some time? Do you feel helpless to escape it? Ignatius answers: Do not remain alone with this. Speak with a competent spiritual person.

A final comment: rules 5 (do not make changes in spiritual desolation) and 13 (speak with a competent spiritual person) together will bring you safely through *any spiritual darkness* you may ever experience. These are two blessed friends for the journey.

13

"I Feel Sad"

First e-mail from Paul to his father:

Hi, Dad. No special reason for writing today—well, maybe there is one. I'm still grateful for our conversations last summer. I'd always hoped that someday we would speak like that, and now we can. It's changed everything in my relationship with you, and I know you feel the same. I'm just glad that we can talk about important things in this way.

Reply from Paul's father, the next day:

Hi, Paul. Yes, this is mutual. I'd always hoped, too, that you and I could share like this. I'm not sure what changed to make it possible. I think it was mostly on my end. Your mother says that it's because I'm more serious about my faith. She may be right. I know that I'm happier since I started praying, or at least trying to. Sometimes it's easier, and at other times it's harder. When you talk about your prayer, it helps me to stay with it. So, this works both ways.

Struggles in the Spiritual Life

Second e-mail from Paul to his father, the next day:

> Thanks for your message and what you say. I imagine that
> we all have these ups and downs in prayer. I know I do. For
> me, recently, prayer has been harder. It's not dramatically
> difficult, it's just less joyful. Sometimes it even feels sad.[17]

Second e-mail from Paul's father, the same day:

> Well, if I can say it, I'm glad to know that I'm not the only
> one who struggles. I'm so new to prayer, I mean personal
> prayer, that I don't understand much about it. I'm trying,
> but I often have questions that I can't answer. You mention
> being sad in prayer. Why do you think that's happening?

Third e-mail from Paul to his father, that evening:

> It's a funny thing, but it's been like this for some weeks, and
> I noticed it only recently. I'm beginning to see the difference
> it makes when you notice what's happening in your prayer.
> The same seems true of your spiritual life as a whole.
>
> Why is it less joyful? Here's one reason. You know that
> I try to find quiet time for prayer every day. Most often, I do
> it early, before leaving for work. If I can't pray then, I do it
> in the school chapel when my teaching allows. I started this
> some years ago, and it really helps me.
>
> During that prayer, sometimes I just want to sit and be
> with the Lord. Maybe I've been praying with a biblical pas-
> sage, but then I put the Bible down, and I'm just there with

---

[17] For what follows, see Gallagher, *Setting Captives Free*, 30–31.

the Lord. It's welcome, and it's happy. Then this thought comes: "You aren't praying. You should be reflecting on the passage or using the time better in some other way. Right now, you're not doing anything. This isn't really prayer." As I said, it's not dramatic, and for a long time, I didn't even notice it. The thought doesn't stop me from praying in that quiet way, but it makes me uneasy and diminishes my joy. That's when the sadness comes.

Third e-mail from Paul's father, the next day:

> Thank you for describing this. But now I'm really confused. The prayer is welcome and happy – then sad. Why should you doubt your prayer? Why do discouraging thoughts like these arise? Can you help me understand? If you, who have been praying for years, have these struggles, what about people like me, who are new to this and know so little?

Fourth e-mail from Paul to his father, that evening:

> I'm not sure how answer your questions. But I can tell you more about what I experience. Maybe it will just confuse things more! Anyway, here goes.
>
> I've noticed another thing. Sometimes when I pray, I want to bring ordinary, daily things to the Lord. I want to talk about them and ask help with them. Maybe it's something in my relationship with Rose, some small tension or a decision we need to make. Maybe it concerns the children or my teaching or projects I have in mind – anything that's part of my daily life. And then a thought comes: "What about the real problems in the world? What about people suffering

91

from wars, earthquakes, and other natural disasters? What
about the people starving, people who have no homes? What
about people battling cancer or other illnesses? Look at you.
Aren't you ashamed to bring such petty things to the Lord?"
Like the other thought, this doesn't stop me, but it dampens
my freedom and joy as I pray.

One final version of this sadness. Saint John of the Cross
says that many reach the threshold of deep prayer but never
cross it. They just remain there, without progressing further.
When prayer is dry and difficult, when I'm distracted, when
I just want the time to be over, there is the thought: "You're
one of those who never cross that threshold. You've been pray-
ing for years, and look at how poorly you do it. Saint John
of the Cross had people like you in mind when he said that.
You're not wholehearted about your prayer, and so you don't
make progress." This thought makes me sad, probably more
than the others I've described.

Fourth e-mail from Paul's father, the next day:

I had no idea that things like this happen when you pray.
How do you understand this sadness? How do you deal
with it?

Fifth e-mail from Paul to his father, that evening:

Those are the right questions. As I said, I'm not sure of the
answers. I do know that something is wrong with this. It
doesn't have the feel of God. I'm sure there are answers, and
I want to find them. The sadness seems to have increased
lately, and it's getting harder to pray.

∞

Yes, those are the right questions, and there are answers. By now, I imagine you can guess what they are!

Before Paul—or we—can answer these questions, we need to identify the sadness he feels. Paul is faithful to prayer and has been for years. He loves it, and he feels its fruits. Though the sadness weighs on him, Paul does not let it stop him. In fact, he is progressing in prayer, as his increased awareness of his experience reveals. Paul now notes spiritual movements, even this undramatic, nonclamorous sense of sadness. He can identify the thoughts from which it originates. Paul's sadness, then, does not derive from negligence on his part.

How, then, should we understand it? Paul experiences a form of spiritual desolation that Ignatius describes as finding oneself "totally sad." Paul is not yet "totally" sad, but things appear to be moving in that direction.

Once again, no shame, so surprise; be aware, identify, reject.

This sadness is distinct from the healthy—even if painful— sadness we feel at the loss of a loved one, the termination of a rewarding occupation, and the like. This is a spiritual sadness with nothing healthy about it. It arises from lies of the enemy. He tells you that you should be ashamed to bring such "small" things to prayer—to the God who knows when a sparrow falls to the ground and counts the hairs on your head (Luke 12:6-7), the God to whom everything in your life is important. The enemy tells you that you are not really praying—when, in reality, God is calling you to a simpler and richer prayer. The enemy tells you that you have stopped at the threshold of deep prayer—when you have only encountered the dry and distracted moments that all who pray faithfully experience. All this is from the liar and father of lies! The only fitting response is to unmask the lies and reject them.

Paul exemplifies well the "awareness" of which Ignatius speaks: he is conscious of his sadness and can identify the thoughts from which it springs. This is the first step toward liberation. He needs help now to understand this sadness for the spiritual desolation it is and to reject it.

What will help us grow in such awareness? Ignatius offers us the *examen prayer*: a brief, daily exercise in which we review the spiritual experiences of the day, consider our response to them, and determine how we can grow in the future. With Ignatius, I warmly recommend the practice of this blessed prayer.[18]

In his fourteenth and final rule, Ignatius supplies yet another tool for rejecting the enemy's desolations and temptations. All of us, you and I, have some point of greatest vulnerability to these tactics of the enemy. There is no shame in this! This is simply what it means to live in a fallen but redeemed and loved world. To identify this point and work to strengthen it is immensely helpful in the spiritual life.

Answers to the following may help us discern this most vulnerable point: What most commonly discourages me in my spiritual life? What most makes me afraid? What most readily strips me of spiritual energy? What makes it hardest to accept God's love and to love Him in return? What most causes me to feel helpless in the spiritual life? And do I see a repeating pattern in this struggle? Our answers may well reveal this place of greatest vulnerability.

---

[18] See Timothy M. Gallagher, OMV, *The Examen Prayer: Ignatian Wisdom for Our Lives Today* (New York: Crossroad, 2006). For podcasts on the examen, see DiscerningHearts.com and the Discerning Hearts app for the series titled The Daily Examen.

Once aware of this point, we can apply spiritual means to strengthen it: prayer in its various forms (Mass, Liturgy of the Hours, Eucharistic Adoration, *lectio divina*, meditation, the Rosary, prayer of petition), conversation with a competent spiritual person (spiritual director, confessor, retreat director, others well formed in the spiritual life), the examen, spiritual reading, and so forth. Progress in this most vulnerable place brings hope where, perhaps, we have long felt most hopeless.

14

"I Feel Alone"

From Cathy's journal, two weeks after the last entry (chapter 10):

> *I have stopped praying. They had a final meeting in the parish when the six weeks of prayer ended. I didn't go. I'm still angry, and I still hurt. It would have been better never to begin the six weeks.*

From Cathy's journal, three days later:

> *All that closeness and warmth of God's love? It's gone like smoke. Maybe it was just feelings and never real. I'm sitting in the kitchen as I write, and I feel like I'm here, and God is a million miles away.*

From Cathy's journal, the next day:

> *I looked again at what I wrote in week six, on the last day I prayed. This was my final sentence: "I need to speak with someone who can help me make sense out of this." Something in me both wants that and rebels against it.*

Struggles in the Spiritual Life

From Cathy's journal, two days later:

> *Just before I stopped praying, I also wrote this: "As I sit here in my room, I don't feel His compassion. I don't feel His closeness. I don't feel His love. He feels distant, like I'm here and He is far away." All of that remains true, except that it's increased. I feel alone, alone, alone, and I hurt.*

E-mail from Cathy to Father Reed, a week later:

> *Dear Father Reed,*
> *My name is Cathy Wilson, and I'm a member of the parish. I need to speak with someone about some spiritual things, and a friend told me that you meet with people. Could I see you when you have time?*
> *Thank you, Cathy*

E-mail from Father Reed to Cathy, the same day:

> *Dear Cathy,*
> *Yes, I'd be happy to meet. I have time in the afternoon on Friday and Saturday. If either works for you, may I suggest 1:00?*
> *Blessings, Father Reed*

E-mail from Cathy to Father Reed, that evening:

> *Dear Father Reed,*
> *Saturday afternoon at 1:00 works well. I will see you then.*
> *Thank you, Cathy*

∞

First meeting of Father Reed and Cathy, Saturday afternoon:

Father Reed welcomed Cathy, and they sat in the rectory parlor. After they introduced themselves, Father Reed prayed briefly and prepared to listen.

"Father," Cathy said, "I'm nervous, and part of me doesn't want to be here at all. I am here because I can't go on the way I have, and I need to talk to someone. My friend mentioned you, and so I've come."

Father Reed nodded and said, "I'm glad you did."

"Maybe the best thing," Cathy said, "would be to describe what I experienced in the six-week program of prayer that Father Bauer led."

"Yes, I think that would be good," Father Reed replied.

"I signed up because I've always wanted to pray with the Bible, but I never knew how. The first weeks were wonderful. I liked the talks, I enjoyed the other people, and I especially loved feeling that I could pray with Scripture. The passages were alive. I felt close to God, and I felt His love. I was also more patient and understanding toward others. I'd say the first three weeks were like that."

Father Reed nodded.

"Here's where it gets harder," Cathy said. "The fourth week was not as warm, but it was not difficult, and I had no trouble persevering. Then we got to the fifth week." She paused.

"Do you want to talk about it?" Father Reed asked. "It's important that you go at your own pace and not force anything."

"Yes, I want to talk about it," Cathy answered, "That's why I'm here."

Father Reed nodded his assent.

"I can tell you the moment that things changed. It was Friday of the fifth week, and the text was the calming of the storm. It began as usual, but when I got to Jesus's question, "Why are you terrified, O you of little faith?" I was completely unprepared for what happened."

Father Reed remained silent, encouraging Cathy to continue.

"His question opened a place in my heart that I had closed years ago — ten years ago, to be exact. That was when I had cancer. I had to have surgery, and it meant that I'd never have children. When I heard Jesus ask the disciples, who were in such terrible danger, why they were afraid, something burst in me. Of course they were afraid! Of course I was afraid ten years ago! And he slept during their storm and mine. The pain and the anger I felt were more intense than I can say." She stopped.

Father Reed remained silent, gazing at her and listening.

"From that moment, the love, the closeness, the sense of growth, the new willingness to help others — all of that disappeared. I've stopped praying because I don't want to keep hurting. I feel like God is far away. I'm alone, angry, and in pain, and I don't know what to do. That's why I'm here."

Father Reed did not speak immediately. "May I ask, Cathy," he said after the pause, "have you ever shared that anger and pain with the Lord? Have you ever spoken with the Lord about it?"

"No," she answered, "I never have. Ten years ago, I didn't know that you could. Now I just don't know what to do. I did get counseling years ago. My family and friends have been supportive, but I've never talked to God about it. Back then, I didn't want to and didn't even know if I should. I would just have expressed anger and pain."

"Would you feel free to express anger and pain to God?"

"I didn't then."

"And now?"

"Can you express anger and pain to God? Anger that He didn't answer when you called, and that there are consequences because he didn't?"

"Yes, Cathy, you can. Don't you think that God wants you to? That he wants you to share what is really in your heart? Isn't that how people grow closer to each other? Think of the Psalms, think of the book of Job, and how often the speakers in those books express what is truly in their hearts, even when it's not pretty. Because they do, things move forward in their relationship with God. Yes, Cathy, you can do that."

She was silent, absorbing the thought.

"My guess," Father Reed said, "is that having talked about this here, you may find it easier to talk about it with the Lord. You could consider trying. If it doesn't feel right, I wouldn't force anything."

"I'll think about it. Would you be open to meeting again if I wanted that?"

"Yes, certainly."

Second meeting of Father Reed and Cathy, three weeks later: After Father Reed's prayer, Cathy said, "I did try to tell God exactly what is in my heart. These weeks of prayer have been the most tumultuous of my life. I'm glad to be praying again, but there have been huge ups and downs. I suppose that's not surprising."

"No, I don't think it is," said Father Reed.

"I looked at the Psalms and Job, and I saw that when the speakers feel that God has treated them unjustly, they simply say it—and very strongly too."

"Yes," Father Reed agreed, "they do."

"It gave me more freedom to tell God what is in my heart and has been there for ten years. I still need more time, maybe a lot of time, but I've made a beginning. I can pray again, and my prayer feels real."

"It is real," said Father Reed. "May I ask, what's your sense of how God responds when you share this way?"

Cathy paused for a moment. "I think," she said, "that he is present to me, that he is glad that I'm telling him what I really feel, and that somehow we grow closer when I do. You know," she added, "I never thought of it till just now, but God doesn't seem so distant anymore."

"It's good to hear that, Cathy."

"Then what about the closeness that I felt with God during the first weeks of the program before any of this happened? Was that real?"

"Yes," said Father Reed, "that was real. It is just because it was so real that this deeper place in your heart was touched and that you can now open it to God. When it was touched, you felt a sense of desolation, of distance from God, of anger and hurt, and that was hard. It could not have been otherwise, given what happened ten years ago. But when you respond as you're doing now—that is, not running but sharing your heart openly with God—then healing begins, and your relationship with God grows.

For a moment, Cathy did not speak. Then she looked at Father Reed. "Thank you," she said quietly.

In a final form of spiritual desolation, Ignatius tells us, a person feels "as if separated from his Creator and Lord." Cathy experiences this strongly in the weeks described: *All that closeness and warmth of God's love? It's gone like smoke.... I'm sitting in the kitchen as I write, and I feel like I'm here, and God is a million miles away.* I'm here, and God is a million miles away. I'm here, sitting in my kitchen, alone in my apartment, commuting to work, driving to pick up the children, sitting at my computer ... and you are a million miles away, distant, remote.

Have you ever felt that? Yes, certainly, you have, and I have. Once more: no shame, no surprise; be aware, identify, reject.

Ignatius advisedly writes "as if separated" because, like every other form of spiritual desolation, this, too, is a lie. God is "Emmanuel," that is, "God with us" (see Matt. 1:23), ever close to us, daily, constantly, with infinite love, even to the end of the age (Matt. 28:20). When Cathy sits in the kitchen, when you drive to work, when you prepare a meal, when you live the hours of the day with its prayer, labor, conversation, and times of rest, God is *always* with you. Saint Augustine affirms that "He is nearer to me than I am to myself,"[19] and in Paul Claudel's lovely expression, God is "Someone in me who is more myself than I am."[20]

In spiritual desolation, however, we *feel* separated, alone, distant from God. If we believe the lie that says, "What you feel is the truth: you *are* distant from God," the desolation will weigh heavily. When we unmask the lie and reject it, we find liberation.

A related quality of spiritual desolation merits note. When we experience such desolation, the enemy insinuates that "it's only you. Others do not struggle with discouragement, the pull of low and earthly things, the lack of hope and of spiritual energy, as you do. Others are not separated from God the way you are. And if they do experience something of this, they overcome it more quickly and more easily than you do. It's just you. You're the only one who struggles this way. You're the only one who feels this discouragement and responds so poorly to it."

[19] Quoted in Fr. Kilian Lynch, O.Carm., "The Practice of the Presence of God," Carmelites, September 5, 2012, https://ocarm.org/en/item/2257.

[20] Quoted in Stephen E. Lewis, "A Fitting Receptacle: Paul Claudel on Poetry and Sensations of God," *Logos* (September 22, 2014), The Free Library, https://www.thefreelibrary.com/A+fitting+receptacle%3A+Paul+Claudel+on+Poetry+and+Sensations+of+God.-a0382318734.

A final time, no! Every autobiography ever written by a saint shows the contrary. Every authentic account of spiritual experience, written or spoken, does likewise. Every man and woman who has ever loved the Lord has experienced spiritual desolation. This is normal in the spiritual life. All of us, you and I, undergo times of spiritual desolation. The call is to perceive the lie and reject it.

∞

In the past chapters, we reviewed the means for rejecting spiritual desolation. I offer here a summary of these means as Ignatius gives them:[21]

- In time of desolation, never make a change.

- Change, rather, how you face the desolation. Turn to prayer of petition, to meditation on spiritual truths and biblical verses that will strengthen you, to examination of what you are experiencing and how it began, to standing your ground with suitable gestures of penitential courage.

- Think about this truth: that though you do not feel it, God is giving you all the grace you need to reject the desolation. Know that you *can* reject it.

- Remain patient, and remember that this desolation will pass and consolation will return—much sooner than the desolation would have you believe.

- Consider that if God permits you to undergo this deso-lation, it is out of love and because of the progress you

---

[21] See Ignatius's rules 5–14 for the discernment of spirits: *Spiritual Exercises*, 318-327.

make when you resist and reject it: healing, growth, and a blessed humility.

• Prepare ahead of time for desolation.

• Be humble in consolation and trusting in desolation.

• Stop the snowball at the top of the mountain! Resist the enemy's temptations and desolations *at their very beginning.*

• Do not remain alone with the enemy's burdens, temptations, and desolations. Speak about these with a wise and competent spiritual person.

• Note where you are most vulnerable to the enemy's temptations and desolations, and strengthen this aspect of your spiritual life.

Jesus said, "The Spirit of the Lord is upon me, because he has anointed me to bring glad tidings to the poor. He has sent me to proclaim liberty to captives and … to let the oppressed go free" (Luke 4:18). Jesus came *to set captives free,* free from the discouraging lies and temptations of the enemy. These Ignatian tools are blessed means toward that freedom.

Part 3

Forms of Dryness

15

A Need for Formation

First e-mail from Paul's father to Paul, three months later (see chapter 13):

> *We've been talking about prayer, and I'm trying, but it's still very new. When I began earlier this year, I started with the Rosary because I remembered it from your grandparents. I struggled with it, got distracted easily, and sometimes found it hard to persevere. But it's what I know, and I think the Lord must be pleased to see me trying, even if it's hard. You've spoken about a quiet time each day to pray with the Bible. I've never done that, and it sounds interesting.*

Second e-mail from Paul's father to Paul, a week later:

> *On Sunday, our pastor talked about praying with the Bible. He invited all of us to do this for ten minutes or more, if we can, each day. In the bulletin, he quoted Saint Francis de Sales, who says, "I especially counsel you to practice mental prayer, the prayer of the heart, and particularly that which centers on the life and passion of the Lord. By often turning your eyes on*

him in meditation, your whole soul will be filled with him.... I
assure you that we cannot go to God the Father except through
this gate."[22] Is this what you've been doing? Maybe I should try
it. This saint makes it sound pretty important.

Third e-mail from Paul's father to Paul, ten days later:

I got a Bible last week, the first one I've ever had. Our pas-
tor mentioned praying with the Gospel from the day's Mass,
and that makes sense to me. I also subscribed to the monthly
publication he mentioned so that I'll know what the day's
Gospel is. I seem now to have what I need. It's probably wise
to stay with ten minutes since this is all new.

Fourth e-mail from Paul's father to Paul, five days later:

Well, this morning I made my first try, ten minutes with the
day's Gospel.[23] The text was Matthew 5:1–12, where Jesus
tells different kinds of people that they are blessed. It says
that He is on a mountain. I don't know where the mountain
is or why He went there. I had all kinds of questions: Who
are these who are poor in spirit? What does that mean?
What is the Kingdom of Heaven? Is that here on Earth or
in Heaven? Why should people who mourn be called blessed?
That's not what we usually think. What are they mourning
about? Who is going to comfort them? I imagine it is God.

---

[22] St. Francis de Sales, *Introduction to the Devout Life*, trans. John K. Ryan (New York: Image, 2014), 70–71.

[23] These readings begin with November 1 and continue with Sunday readings from year B and with daily readings from year 1.

And so on for ten minutes. It passed quickly, but I had more questions than answers. Still, I'm glad to have begun.

Fifth e-mail from Paul's father to Paul, three days later:

This is my third day, and the Gospel for today is Luke 14:25–33. It puzzles me that I started with Matthew 5 two days ago, and now the Gospel is Luke 14. Why does it skip around like this? Right away, I had a question: Why does Jesus tell us that we have to hate our parents, our children, and our brothers and sisters if we want to be his disciples? I thought we were supposed to love, not hate. Then he talks about building towers and going to battle. I suppose that, like anything new, it takes time to understand all this.

Sixth e-mail from Paul's father to Paul, a week later:

I've been doing these ten minutes after supper, but I often get interrupted. Somebody calls, or your mother says something, or the television is on. To be honest, I'm finding this prayer hard. I can't seem to get into it. Today's Gospel was Luke 17:11–19, about lepers, Samaria, Galilee, being healed, and some priests. I got a vague sense that we should thank God for his blessings, but there's a lot I don't understand. I'm beginning to wonder if I can keep this up. Not much happens when I try to pray in this way.

Seventh e-mail from Paul's father to Paul, four days later:

More questions about the Gospel, Mark 13:24–32. "In those days": What days are these? What tribulation? Why

will the sun be darkened and the moon not give light? Then
the Son of Man coming on clouds, fig trees, and an hour
that no one knows. I don't know how to put this together
with Saint Francis de Sales's words about how important
meditation is. I just know that I don't find it helpful. I'm
reluctant to do it when I know it will be dry and difficult.

∞

Paul's father begins a new practice of prayer—meditation on Scripture—with goodwill. He has heard in preaching and from a saint that this is important and fruitful. He acquires a Bible and a publication with the readings, and he sets aside time. He begins and finds that his prayer is *dry*, so much that he considers abandoning it.

Paul's father's dryness in prayer does not arise from any fault on his part. On the contrary, he is diligent in preparing and approaches his prayer with goodwill. It derives, rather, from a lack of formation in prayer. Signs of this abound. When Paul's father begins to pray, he chooses the Rosary because he saw his parents pray it. He knows little about the Rosary beyond its mechanics and, understandably, is easily distracted when he prays it.

Paul's father has never read the Bible. He has no formation in Scripture and, again unsurprisingly, struggles to comprehend it. When he tries to meditate, he encounters more questions than spiritual insight. He does not understand why given Gospel passages are chosen for given days. With good intentions but unwisely, he chooses a time and place that render prayer difficult. Most likely, if Paul's father continues to pray in this way, his prayer will be dry. Even more likely, he will not persevere.

This will change when he receives formation in prayer. Bible study will help him to understand the texts and so permit them to nourish him spiritually. Parish classes on prayer; spiritual books about meditation; resources on the web; meetings with a spiritual director, if possible; conversation with Paul, who is more experienced in prayer—all this will prepare Paul's father to meditate fruitfully. As his schooling in prayer deepens, his meditation will no longer be dry. The Rosary, too, understood as contemplation of Jesus, will be less distracted. *Formation in prayer* resolves this form of dryness.

Would additional formation in prayer help you? You are not new to prayer, like Paul. Nonetheless, further formation—learning from figures of holiness and wisdom in our spiritual tradition—will very likely enhance your prayer. We may find dryness diminish as we learn more about prayer.

16

Something Has Slipped

It was Saturday afternoon, and Julie and Emily had met for coffee. The shop was crowded and noisy, and they preferred to sit outside under the awning. They had not seen each other for some months, and they welcomed the time together. Their conversation flowed naturally until it turned, as it always did when they spoke, to spiritual things.

"You've become a little quiet," Emily said. "Is something on your mind?"

Julie smiled. "You know me too well," she said, "and I can't hide much from you."

"I'm guessing that it's something about prayer? When we began to talk about that, you grew silent."

"It is about prayer. But to tell you about it, I'll have to go back a few months."

"That's why we're here, isn't it? To share."

Julie nodded. "Yes," she said, "and I've wanted to talk about this. If you're willing to listen, I'll tell you what's happened."

She thought for a moment, and then said, "Four months ago, our parish hosted a weekend on prayer. A speaker came and talked about Saint Ignatius of Loyola's approach to praying with the Bible.

You can either reflect on the meaning of the words or, if there is an event in the passage, imagine yourself in it and taking part. It was all new to me, and I liked it. The speaker gave concrete advice from Saint Ignatius on how to prepare for prayer, how to enter it, what to do as you pray with the passage, and how to end the prayer. For the first time, I felt like I could actually pray with the Bible."

Emily nodded, "Yes, I remember when you wrote to me about that."

"So, I started doing what the speaker suggested. In the evening, I looked at the readings for the next day's Mass. I chose the one that most spoke to me, either the First Reading, the Psalm, or the Gospel. The app I use gives you a brief commentary, and I read that. I found that Saint Ignatius's advice about preparing the evening before makes a difference. Because the prayer is prepared and not last-minute, you enter it more easily."

Emily nodded again.

"I made a few adjustments to my evening routine to get the sleep I need and still have twenty minutes for prayer in the morning before the activity starts. Basically, it meant less time watching television and on the Internet. So, it was not hard to get that time in the morning.

"I also found helpful Saint Ignatius's counsel to begin the prayer by seeing the love in Jesus's eyes as he looks upon me. It made the prayer relational from the start—not me and a book, but me and a Person, Jesus. I liked doing this."

"It sounds like that weekend was really helpful," Emily said.

"It was. When it finished, I told Bob, 'Someone has finally taught me how to pray.' This approach made a real difference, and I found prayer more alive than ever before. I don't have the words for it," Julie continued, "but you know how, when you're really praying, and you do it day after day, week after week, something changes in your relationship with God. Your faith comes more alive. God is more real, more present during the day. You have more peace. People start to see a difference. After I'd been doing this a few months, Bob told me that he could see the change, and he loved it. I think the children felt it too."

"Yes," Emily said, "I know what you mean."

"But recently it's gotten harder to pray. The prayer seems more dry. I get distracted more easily. It doesn't have the same impact. Some days, I don't pray. I'm not happy about it, but that's where things are. And that's why I got silent when you began talking about prayer."

"What's happened?" Emily asked. "Has anything changed in these last weeks?"

"Nothing major," Julie replied.

"What about small changes, then?" Emily said. "Have there been any of those?"

Julie thought and then smiled a little wryly. "I'm almost ashamed to tell you, but I've gotten interested in that new TV series. Once I started watching it, I've been spending more time on TV most evenings."

"Why does that come to mind?"

"Because it has changed my evenings. I get to bed later now."

"How does that affect things?"

"In two ways. It's harder to get up early and have that time for prayer. So, some days I do the twenty minutes whenever I can, and it's usually more distracted. Also, it means that I don't prepare the same way in the evening. I look at the readings quickly, if I do at all, and I don't always get to the commentary."

"I can see how that makes a difference."

"It does, and when I go to pray, I feel that I'm not prepared, and so it's harder to get started. I also feel less free to see the Lord's look of love as I begin, before I immerse myself in the passage."

Julie looked at Emily. "To be honest," she said, "there's no great mystery here. If I return to the way I prepared before and if I pray in the morning, I don't doubt that the dryness will pass, and that prayer will be fruitful again."

In this experience of dryness, the issue is negligence regarding prayer. The solution is to reverse that negligence. We all have routines, times of day, ways of choosing material, places, and the like that we know help us to pray. When we are faithful to them, this form of dryness resolves.

17

Inconsistency

From John's journal, one year after the last entry (chapter 7):

> *Prayer continues to be blessed. I have reached Matthew*
> *5, the Sermon on the Mount, and today, "Love your*
> *enemies." This verse caught my attention, and it made*
> *me think. Do I have enemies? Are there people I have not*
> *forgiven?*
>
> *I can see places where I need to change. What is new is*
> *that I really want to make the change. I'll talk with Jennie*
> *about my relationship with her family.*

From John's journal, two weeks later:

> *Matthew 7:7: "Ask and it will be given to you." I spent the*
> *prayer focusing on this sentence. I encounter things in the*
> *spiritual life that I feel I can't do, that I'm too inconstant,*
> *too weak, too easily discouraged. But this I can always do: I*
> *can ask. It was a good time of prayer, and it leaves me with*
> *greater confidence.*

Struggles in the Spiritual Life

From John's journal, one month later:

> Matthew 9:13: "I desire mercy, not sacrifice. I did
> not come to call the righteous but sinners." Another
> word of consolation. It gives me greater courage in my
> struggles.

From John's journal, three weeks later:

> The final part of Matthew 10, where Jesus asks that no
> relationship be placed above our relationship with him,
> was not easy for me.

From John's journal, two weeks later:

> Matthew 11 doesn't speak to me the way the earlier chap-
> ters did: people did not receive John the Baptist, the towns
> were unrepentant, things are hidden from the wise and
> learned. I continue with this morning time, but I don't look
> forward to it as much.

From John's journal, one day later:

> Prayer is still empty, even hard. It's time to be honest.
> Matthew 11 is difficult for me because this chapter makes
> me face a conflict. It has to do with Sheila, my assistant,
> who began working with me two months ago. It's hard
> even to write this, and it troubles me, but I'm drawn
> to her in a way that could end badly. I try to keep it in
> check, and I hope she doesn't notice anything, but she
> might.

Inconsistency

From John's journal, two weeks later:

> Matthew 12 is just as hard as Matthew 11: Pharisees complaining and resisting, trees with bad fruit, your own words condemn you. I find it difficult to pray, and not much seems to happen—except that the same thing surfaces and troubles me: Sheila. I joined her for lunch today in the cafeteria. I knew that, feeling as I do, I should not have. It's not right. I try not to show it, but my guess is that she knows.

From John's journal, one week later:

> Matthew 13 is no easier: seed on the path, on rocky ground, among thorns. Prayer continues to be dry and troubled. I can't go on like this. Today I saw clearly that prayer is leading me in one direction, closer to the Lord, to Jennie, to my children, and to the Church, and this attraction for Sheila is pulling me in a different direction. Jesus, you told us to ask. I am asking now. I need you. I can't do it without you.

From John's journal, three weeks later:

> I spoke with Father Reed today, and it was a relief to talk about this. We worked out what I need to do about Sheila. I'll do it. Father and I will meet in a few weeks to see how it's going. For the first time in recent months, I feel better.

From John's journal, one week later:

> Matthew 14: Jesus gets out of the boat, sees the crowd, is moved with compassion for them, and heals them. It was

*an encouraging time of prayer. I feel like He is doing this
for me as well. I've been faithful to what Father Reed and I
planned when we spoke, and it's making a difference. I think
Sheila is aware of the change, and my sense is that she, too,
is relieved. The boundaries are clearer now, and everything
goes better when they are.*

From John's journal, two weeks later:

*Matthew 15: the Canaanite woman's faith. She just keeps
asking, and her prayer is heard. My heart was lifted as I
prayed with this passage. I feel like my prayer of some weeks
ago is being heard. I met with Father Reed today, and he
was happy to hear how things are going. I feel whole again.*

∞

In the early weeks of this sequence, John's prayer is warm and
uplifting: "*Love your enemies*"; "*Ask and it will be given to you*"; "*I
desire mercy, not sacrifice.*" Then his prayer changes: "*The final part
of Matthew 10, where Jesus asks that no relationship be placed above our
relationship with him, was not easy for me.*"

The change is accentuated in subsequent weeks: "*Matthew 11
doesn't speak to me the way the earlier chapters did*"; "*I don't look forward
to prayer as much these days*"; "*Prayer is still empty, even hard*"; "*I find it
difficult to pray, and not much seems to happen*"; "*Prayer continues to be
dry and troubled.*" As John says, his prayer has become dry. The earlier
warmth has disappeared. Now prayer feels empty, difficult, hard.

After some weeks, John understands why his prayer is dry and is
honest enough to admit it: "*Matthew 11 is difficult for me because this
chapter makes me face a conflict. It has to do with Sheila, my assistant.*"

Yes, John's prayer obliges him to face an emerging inconsistency between his prayer and his life: "*Today I saw clearly that prayer is leading me in one direction, closer to the Lord, to Jennie, to my children, and to the Church, and this attraction for Sheila is pulling me in a different direction.*"

While the inconsistency persists, John's prayer is dry, troubling, and conflicted. When, with the help of prayer and conversation with Father Reed, the inconsistency resolves, the dryness dissipates. Prayer is once again warm: "*Matthew 14: Jesus gets out of the boat, sees the crowd, is moved with compassion for them, and heals them. It was an encouraging time of prayer*"; "*Matthew 15: the Canaanite woman's faith. She just keeps asking, and her prayer is heard. My heart was lifted as I prayed with this passage.*"

Inconsistencies between our prayer and our lives will cause dryness in prayer: a refusal to forgive, firmly guarded anger, all-encompassing pursuit of material goals, self-centeredness, harmful relationships, and so forth. As these areas of our lives are brought to Christ and healed, dryness in prayer lifts.

Of the time before her profound conversion, Saint Teresa of Avila writes, "I began to return to prayer without, however, removing the occasions of sin.... My life was very hard, because in prayer I understood my faults more clearly."[24] When that conversion occurred, the dryness passed, and her prayer blossomed in a way that continues to bless the Church.

The dryness caused by inconsistency between prayer and life is, at root, a loving call from God to healing and to new life.

---

[24] *Life*, 7, 17. Author's translation.

18

Growth

E-mail from Cathy to Father Reed, three months after their last meeting (chapter 14):

> I want to thank you for again for meeting with me. It was a great help, and, as I told you, I'm able to pray again. It has remained tumultuous, but gradually I find it easier to share with God that place of pain and anger. And the really good thing is that, when I do, I feel less hurt, less angry, and less alone. That isn't quite right: I don't feel alone anymore on that deep level.
>
> I'm able again to use the ways of praying that Father Bauer taught us in those six weeks: choosing the Scripture the night before, seeing Jesus's look of love as I begin, and reflecting on the passage or imagining myself present in the scene. It is welcome to pray this way again. It saves me from wandering and not knowing how to proceed.
>
> I choose one of the readings from the day's Mass. I pray first thing in the morning, sometimes for a half hour. On Saturdays, I spend an hour in the Adoration chapel at the parish, and I find the setting helpful.

> *I want to thank you for helping me to pray again and to let you know that things are progressing. With my thanks, Cathy*

E-mail from Father Reed to Cathy, the next day:

> *I'm happy to hear all that you share. It is wonderful that you are praying so faithfully. God's grace is at work as you do. I am especially glad to hear that your relationship with God is growing and that you no longer feel alone. May God continue this work of growth in you. With my prayers, Father Reed*

From Cathy's journal, two months later, Saturday morning in the Adoration chapel:

> *I spent the hour with today's First Reading, Deuteronomy 6:4–13, especially the beginning: "The LORD is our God, the LORD alone! Therefore, you shall love the LORD, your God, with your whole heart, and with your whole being, and with your whole strength." The hour felt blessed and passed almost before I knew it. God's unique place in my life, the Lord alone. And then a love for Him that is total, with all of me, my whole heart, being, and strength. Just these few words from the reading, but they said so much, everything. I thought about them—with my heart and from my heart. I leave this hour feeling close to God.*

From Cathy's journal, the following Tuesday:

> *Today's Gospel is John 12, for the memorial of Saint Lawrence: "Unless a grain of wheat falls to the ground*

and dies, it remains just a grain of wheat; but if it dies,
it produces much fruit." I thought of planting seeds in our
garden, watching them die in order to bring forth new life.
Is that why the Lord permitted the cancer those years ago?
I spoke with the Lord about this. I don't have answers,
but something in me grew more hopeful as I shared with
the Lord.

Does this mean that the Lord is bringing forth new life in
me and through me for others? Is that what the Lord wants
to tell me this morning?

From Cathy's journal, the following Saturday in the Adoration
chapel:

I chose the Gospel, Matthew 19:13-15, about the mothers
who bring their children to Jesus. I hesitated to choose this
passage because it touches that place that still hurts, that
longs for the children I can never have. But I think it was
the right choice.

I was there, in the scene, standing near Jesus, watching
as each mother brought her child to him. I watched him
speak with the children and their mothers and bless them.
Something in me hurt: I was a bystander. I had no children
to bring.

But I was able to stay there, and somehow, I knew
that Jesus wanted me there, that he knew my sorrow, that
it mattered to him, and that he would not leave me alone.
Somewhere in my heart, I heard him say that he would bring
life from my life, even from my pain. There were tears in this
prayer, tears from a deep place, but they were not bitter, and
I was not alone.

Struggles in the Spiritual Life

∞

Two years later.

From Cathy's journal, Monday morning:

> Today's Gospel was Luke 5:17–26. Jesus forgives the
> paralytic his sins and then heals his physical illness. I looked
> forward to praying with this passage when I chose it last
> evening. I tried to be there in the scene, beside Jesus in the
> house. But, as often happens now, this way of praying didn't
> seem to help, the way it used to. I couldn't visualize the scene
> very well, even though I tried. There were many people there
> and many actions: the packed house, the opening of the roof,
> the lowering of the paralytic, Jesus's forgiving his sins, and
> then the physical healing.
>
> I found that I didn't want to imagine all that movement.
> The scene was busier than I wanted, somehow. Something
> doesn't seem to be working when I pray the way I've prayed
> the past two years. I'm not sure why. I wonder, am I doing
> something wrong? I don't think so. I'm just doing what I
> learned from Father Bauer and what has helped so much in
> these years.

From Cathy's journal, the next morning:

> I thought it might be easier if I didn't try to imagine a scene,
> so I took the First Reading, Isaiah 40:1–11, and especially
> the first words: "Comfort, give comfort to my people. . . .
> Speak to the heart of Jerusalem. . . ." It is a beautiful text,
> and I hoped it would help me pray, just thinking about those
> words. But it didn't. It felt like work, "busier" than I wanted
> to be in prayer. So I wandered and wound up distracted.

What is wrong? This way of praying has been so fruitful; it's so solidly rooted in the Church's tradition. Why doesn't it help me as it used to?

From Cathy's journal, the next morning:

The Gospel was the Annunciation, in Luke 1. I tried the imaginative approach, being there with Mary, and at times I felt like my heart was there, and I could share as Mary spoke with the angel. Yet this time, too, it wasn't as before. It felt busy again, like more activity than I want.

But I keep trying, even though I find myself tired and distracted. My prayer, after being fruitful these past years, is now more dry. Maybe I'm at fault in some way, Probably I am, but I don't know how. At one point in the prayer, I let the imagining go and just sat with the Lord. That felt better. But I'm not sure that's really prayer. I wasn't doing anything. At least, I wasn't doing the things Father Bauer taught us and that have worked so well. It's confusing.

Yes, this situation can be confusing. What is happening in Cathy's prayer? It has become dry. Is this because she lacks formation (chapter 15), has grown negligent (chapter 16), or has permitted an inconsistency between her life and prayer (chapter 17)? None of this appears to be present: Cathy has received formation in prayer, is faithful to it, and shows no sign of inconsistency between her life and prayer.

Yet her prayer is dry. Something else, then, is at work, and in this case, something blessed. Cathy finds herself less drawn than before to reflect on or imagine a scriptural text. She esteems this way of praying and has found it fruitful in the past. Now, however, when she reflects or imagines, she says that "*it felt like work, 'busier' than I wanted to be in prayer.*" On the other hand, at one point "*I let the imagining go and just sat with the Lord. That felt better.*"

Very likely, Cathy's prayer is simplifying. At times, her heart desires to relinquish the "busyness" of reflecting and imagining and simply be with the Lord, her heart with his heart, with little activity, simply together in a blessed and loving communion. She fears that when she gives her heart this freedom, she is not really praying—not thinking about the meaning of a text or participating imaginatively as it unfolds.

On the contrary! Cathy, and anyone in her situation, needs to know that this silent, loving communion is genuine prayer. It is closeness to God and richly fruitful, as when two friends, two spouses, or two siblings cease to speak and are simply present to each other, without exterior activity, without words, needing no words, simply happy to be together. Through the time they spend in this way, they grow in mutual love and communion. The same is true of quiet, silent, loving prayer of this kind.

Cathy does not understand what is happening in her prayer. Confused, she turns to what has helped her in prayer thus far: active reflection or imagining of a scriptural text. When she does, however, it feels like "work" and "busier" than she wants to be. Instead, her heart desires simply to be with the Lord in silent, loving communion. When she does pray this way, it feels better—that is, she is following the Lord's leading in her prayer. What Cathy calls dryness is really a grace-filled call to a quieter form of prayer. If she speaks with Father Reed, he will help her understand this. Then she will follow this call with freedom, joy, and growth.

When this "dryness" is truly a call to rest with the Lord in quiet communion, the person will experience the prayer as warm, relational, and loving. If, upon ceasing the reflective or imaginative activity in prayer, the person experiences emptiness and distractions, he or she should resume that reflective or imaginative activity. Attractions to reflective-imaginative or quiet pray may, at times, alternate in the same person. In each case, he or she is free and does well to follow that attraction.

Cathy's "dryness" reveals that her prayer is growing. She is doing nothing wrong—on the contrary. She needs only to welcome God's loving call when she prays. In similar circumstances, the same is true for us.

19

A Need to Share

Paul and his father sat side by side. The lake before them sparkled in the early morning sun. Their kayaks lay on the shore a few feet away. Paul and his family had joined his parents for a vacation weekend. This morning, Paul and his father had risen early and kayaked as the sun rose. Now they were resting before the paddle back. Both welcomed the time together.

For some minutes, their conversation ranged over matters of the family. Then, as happened often these days, they spoke of mutual experiences of prayer.

"When we last talked," Paul said, "you mentioned that recently prayer had become difficult."

"Yes," his father replied, "and I'm not sure why. As I've learned more about prayer and how to understand the Bible, it's been getting easier. I have more answers to my questions and a better sense of how to proceed."

"But what's happening now?"

"I don't know. I feel like I don't have anything to say to the Lord. It's hard to be in prayer, and the time passes slowly, sometimes very slowly. I get distracted, and nothing seems to help. The life seems to have gone out of the prayer."

They discussed prayer for a time. The conversation moved to other topics, and neither was in a hurry to leave. Then his father said, "Paul, I have something to tell you." Paul looked at his father. The tenseness in his face told Paul that this was not easy for him. Paul nodded, and remained silent, ready to listen.

"The happiest thing in my life recently is our new relationship. You know how much that means to me."

"Yes, I do, and you know how much it means to me."

"Yes, Paul, I do. And because we're closer now, I don't want to hide anything from you. I never thought I could tell you about this—I thought it would break our relationship if I did. It's still very hard, but I'm going to tell you, and I'll accept your response, whatever it is. I told your mother that I would share this with you, and she agreed."

Paul continued to listen, uncertain of what his father would say. He understood now that it was serious.

"You know that for many years, I was far from the Church and from God. I left all that to your mother, and, thankfully, it was in good hands. But I took no part in it."

"Yes, I know," Paul said, "and that's why what's happening now is so special to me."

"There was another part that you don't know. It was when I was working for the insurance company. I had a client, a married woman. Over the months of working together, we began to get mutually attracted. Eventually, it became an affair. It continued, off and on, for about a year. I hid it—or I thought I did—from your mother. It ended when the woman and her family moved to another part of the country. It didn't end by my choice, but it did stop and never resumed."

Paul remained silent, listening.

"I said nothing about this to your mother until last year. I had returned to the Church and wanted to get right with God. I knew that I had to tell her."

Paul nodded. Some things he had noticed between his parents began to make sense.

"I don't have to tell you how hard it was for her and how ashamed I feel. We're dealing with this, but it's taking work. Marriage therapy helped, and we made a retreat for married couples. That was a blessing, and it made a difference. We are committed to each other, and we'll get through it. But it's not been easy."

Paul's father stopped speaking and looked at the water before them. He waited.

For almost a minute, Paul remained silent. Then he said, "Thanks, Dad, for telling me. I can only imagine how hard it was for you to say that. I'll be honest: it will take time to absorb this, and I don't know where my thoughts will go. What I can say is this: what has grown between us is important, and I don't want it to end. If you and Mom are working through this, then you and I can work with it too."

Paul's father turned to him. "That's all and more than I can ask," he said quietly. "Thank you."

E-mail from Paul's father to Paul, five months later:

I appreciated your phone call last Sunday. I know these months have not been easy, and that conversation meant a lot to me. It means a lot to your mother as well. I'm beginning to hope that we'll all be closer than we were before, maybe ever before. That secret weighed on us, all of us. I call it a secret, but it wasn't really. I knew about it, and your mother was aware of something. It troubled her, too, over the years. And I was always afraid of what it would do to us as father and son.

So, two things to say. One is "Thank you," maybe the biggest thank-you I've ever said. The other is this: there are no more secrets. Now you know everything important about me as a husband and father. There won't be any other secrets to share. Everything is out there now.

E-mail from Paul to his father, that evening:

Yes, I'm glad, too, that there are no more secrets. Thank you, and this is a big thank-you on my part too. You mean more to me now than you ever did before.

E-mail from Paul to his father, a month later:

I've been thinking about how you described your prayer when we went kayaking last summer. You've also expressed it recently, how you feel that you don't have anything to say to the Lord, that the life has gone out of your prayer, that it's mostly distractions, and nothing seems to help.

Whenever I bring up problems in prayer, Father Reed always asks me if I've talked to the Lord about it. We smile about it now, because I can almost tell him when he's going to say it. But he's right, and it does make a difference when I share what's in my heart openly with the Lord.

You did that with me last summer: you spoke openly about the secret. It wasn't easy, and we've had to struggle, but both of us are glad now that you took the risk and spoke with me as you did. We wouldn't want to go back to the secrets.

If you were here and met with Father Reed, I know he'd ask you the same thing: Have you talked about the secret with the Lord? I wonder what would happen to the dryness in prayer you describe if you did. You and I have been getting closer, and that's why you needed to speak openly. You and the Lord have been getting closer too. Maybe this kind of sharing has become necessary there too.

E-mail from Paul's father to Paul, the next day:

No, I never have talked about this with the Lord. I spoke about it in Confession when I came back to the Church, but I've never brought it to my prayer. Before, I didn't know that you could do this. Now I know that you can. But I've been too ashamed. I think, though, that something has changed. As I read your e-mail and thought about it, I realized that I'm not so ashamed anymore. I think that speaking with your mother and with you will make it easier to do it with the Lord. I'll try. Maybe that's the next step toward real freedom from this burden.

E-mail from Paul's father to Paul, two weeks later:

Well, I've done my best to share it with the Lord. One thing I can say immediately: prayer isn't dry anymore. There have been ups and downs, times of pain, and even tears, something rare for me. I think that your Father Reed is on target. It wasn't that I had nothing to say to the Lord. It was that I wasn't saying the things I really needed to say. I don't think prayer will be dry in that same way again.

∞

A husband and wife sit at the supper table. A deep love unites them. She carries a burden in her heart, and he, knowing her well, perceives it. But she says nothing about it. They speak as they share the meal: matters of the day, practical questions, comments on the news or about a neighbor. The conversation continues, but both sense something superficial about it, the absence of a deeper communication, the avoiding of what they most need to share.

This pattern continues for some weeks. Then, the day comes when she, with some effort, shares the burden that weighs on her: an issue of health, a hurt in their relationship, a worry about a family situation. The conversation is difficult, at least initially. But now the superficiality is gone. Both speak from the heart. They know that the communication is real and focused on the necessary thing. As they work through the issue, they grow closer together. Something blessed enters their relationship.

Most fundamentally, prayer is a relationship: the human person and the Divine together, in communication. Dryness may arise in prayer when we need to share something with the Lord but have not done so. We may feel ashamed, too angry, too hurt. And so we do not speak of it. Then our prayer feels superficial, dry. We have little to say. Little! The contrary is true: prayer is dry because we have so much to say and have not said it. Father Reed's question is the right one: "Have you spoken about this with the Lord?"

The Jesus who speaks so sensitively with the Samaritan woman (John 4:4–42), who meets with the nervous Nicodemus by night (John 3:1–2), who invites the two saddened disciples to tell him their burdens (Luke 24:13–35), who approaches the weeping Mary Magdalene and pronounces her name (John 20:16), who heals Peter's threefold denial with the threefold question about love

(John 21:15-17): this Jesus never "bulldozes" into human hearts. He is patient (Matt. 12:20) and gentle (Matt. 11:29). But he loves us too much to leave us alone with our fear and shame. He invites us to share the burden with him, to tell him about it, to allow him to accompany us in it. When we do, this form of dryness will pass, and prayer will flow.

Paul's father, in his different context, experiences something of what Cathy experienced (chapter 14). She had never spoken with the Lord about her cancer and its consequences. When she does share her anger and pain with the Lord, prayer opens for her again, and she no longer feels alone.

If there is in your heart a place of pain, anger, hurt, shame, or fear, do not remain alone with it. Hear the invitation of the Jesus, who is gentle and lowly of heart: "Come to me, all you who labor and are burdened, and I will give you rest" (Matt. 11:28). And your prayer will no longer be dry.

20

Image of God

First e-mail from Bob to his brother, one year after his conversation with Julie (chapter 11):

> You know that I've been thinking for some time about the Spiritual Exercises in daily life. Well, I've finally started. I met with my director for the first time this week. He's asking me to spend an hour in prayer every day with Bible texts that he gives me. He also wants me to do some journaling about my prayer when I finish the hour. We'll meet once a week during this process, and this will continue for six or seven months. I've wanted to grow in prayer, and I think this will really help. I'll let you know how it goes.

Second e-mail from Bob to his brother, one week later:

> The Scriptures for prayer have all been about God's love, a welcome place to start. Today, I prayed with Psalm 139:1–18, God's closeness, God at the origin of my being. It's still new but in a good way. I've never spent a full hour in prayer

before, and I welcome the stretch. Thus far, it hasn't been too
hard, and it seem fruitful.

Third e-mail from Bob to his brother, one month later:

At this stage of the Exercises, we pray for increasing freedom
from sin. Today, I prayed with the sin of Adam and Eve in
Genesis 3 and all the harm that came from it. I have to say
that it's getting harder for me to pray. I found the way their
sin was punished troubling. After I prayed with their sin, I
was supposed to see Jesus on the Cross and how He loved me
enough to die for me and save me from this. It didn't turn
out that way. I just keep feeling uneasy. I'll talk about this
when I meet my director.

Fourth e-mail from Bob to his brother, a week later:

My director kept me praying with Genesis 3, and he encour-
ages me to stay with it even though he knows it's hard. He
tells me to go gently, not to force anything, but not to avoid
it either. The same with Jesus on the Cross. He also gave me
Romans 7:14–25, Paul's struggle about not doing the good
that he wants but doing the bad that he does not want. It's
all getting somewhat heavy.

Fifth e-mail from Bob to his brother, three days later:

I'm still praying with the same theme. It's supposed to be
about freedom from sin and God's mercy, but that's not the
experience. At this point, it's all dry, all difficult. I don't
want to make the hour of prayer. When I do, I'm unsettled,

I'm distracted, and God seems distant. I'm committed to this process, so I show up, and I try, but nothing moves me very much. It's discouraging. Maybe I'm not made for this. Maybe I'm overreaching myself spiritually.

Sixth e-mail from Bob to his brother, four days later:

Yesterday, things got heavy. I say and I believe that God is loving, but I don't feel it. As I was praying about sin, it hit me that I've felt like this before. You know my relationship with Dad. I respect him, and I know he loves us, but he could be hard on us. Do you remember the report card when all the grades were good except for the B-, and that was the only grade he mentioned? And the sports car we bought and were trying to repair. I'm not good at that, but I was part of the project, so I had to try. I worked on the body and didn't mix the materials right. Everything had to be done over. I still remember his disgust and his comments. These are only two of many incidents like this. Praying about my sin and the Cross feels like this again: I don't measure up. How can God be pleased with that? The Cross feels less like love and mercy and more like having to face my failures.

Seventh e-mail from Bob to his brother, two days later:

Yesterday, I met with my director. He wondered if I might be projecting onto God my relationship with Dad: unless I did things perfectly, I'd be made to feel it. This was completely new to me. My director asked if I'd ever spoken to God about my relationship with Dad, if I'd ever shared with God that mixture of love, respect, nervousness, and interior pain.

*I never have. He asked if I'd be willing to try. I didn't know.
I answered that I could at least ask God for the grace to do
this. The director encouraged me to do so and suggested that
I pray with Mark 1:11, "You are my beloved Son; with you I
am well pleased," and that I hear the Father say these words
to me.*

Eighth email from Bob to his brother, a week later:

*I've spent the whole week with Mark 1:11. I can't move past
it, and I don't want to. It's been an emotional week. For
the first time, I have spoken to God about my relationship
with Dad. There was more pain than I realized, and I was
surprised to feel anger as well. The new thing is that God
doesn't seem to react the way Dad did, that when I share my
failures, my self-doubt, my limitations, and my sins, there is
no belittling, no scorn, no rejection. He's just there, listening,
welcoming, understanding, wanting to heal. It may be that
I'm understanding the Cross for the first time, I mean really
understanding it. Prayer still isn't entirely easy, but it's not
dry anymore.*

Ninth e-mail from Bob to his brother, a month later:

*The old patterns resurface at times as I pray: God is a father
who watches for faults, for sins, who shames me, who makes
me face my failures. But something is changing. I didn't realize that I saw God the Father so much in the image of Dad.
When I think about it, how could it be otherwise? That was
my experience of fatherhood. It was all I knew. Now that
I'm starting to separate the two, I can begin at least to let*

God the Father be the Father that He really is. My director continues to give me Scriptures about God as Father and His love for me. I'm praying with the life of Jesus, and my director has given me several passages in which Jesus speaks about the love between Him and His Father. From this, I have a new grasp of what it means to be a son – a beloved son – of this Father. "With you I am well pleased": these words mean more and more to me.

Tenth email from Bob to his brother, three months later:

I'm near the end of the Exercises. Remember when I thought, some months ago, that this wasn't for me? I see now that the issue was my need to discover God as He really is, that He is not what I thought. The difference changes everything. Prayer has been happier in these past weeks, and I think that something has changed in a lasting way. I have more to learn, more growth to attain, but I feel that now I can really meet God and talk to Him.

I've shared all this with Julie. I told her that I also want to speak with Dad when the time is right, and she agrees. I hope that something new can happen in our relationship. Dad's been through a lot in these past years, too, and the time might be right. If so, it would be a blessed fruit of these Exercises.

When Bob perceives that his image of God differs from the biblical image of God, his prayer ceases to be dry. He is now free to meet God as He is: loving, close, understanding, merciful, encouraging – the heavenly Father whom Jesus reveals to us.

Through no fault of his own, Bob has absorbed an image of God as a demanding Father, quick to note faults, impatient, ready to criticize. Bob is not aware of this image, but it burdens his relationship with God, and so his prayer.

When he prays with Genesis 3, Bob focuses on *"all the harm that came from"* this sin and *"the way their sin was punished."* The message of mercy in that same chapter (Gen. 3:15) and, above all, in the Cross do not speak to him, and his prayer leaves him uneasy. He describes Romans 7:14–25 as *"Paul's struggle about not doing the good that he wants but doing the bad that he does not want,"* again overlooking the message of freedom with which the passage concludes (Rom. 7:25). When he tries to pray, Bob writes, *"I'm unsettled, I'm distracted, and God seems distant.... I try, but nothing moves me very much. It's discouraging. Maybe I'm not made for this."* Bob's prayer is dry.

His prayer changes when Bob realizes that God is different—more loving, warm, close—than his image of God had led him to believe. Conversation with his director, prayer on biblical passages that reveal God as a loving Father, and his willingness—not without struggle—to share with God his experience of human fatherhood and the mixture of goodness and pain found in it, begin to set Bob free. Now he can meet his heavenly Father as God really is. Now a relationship based on a true image of the Father can develop. Now he knows himself to be a beloved son of this Father. Now his prayer is not dry.

A person's image of God may be one cause of dryness. In Bob's case, this arises from an imperfect experience of fatherhood in light of which he sees God. Other experiences may also cause a dissonance between God as he is and a person's image of him. There is no shame in this! There is no guilt in this. Awareness of this dissonance, however, opens a door to blessed growth. Conversation with a competent spiritual person, prayer with well-chosen passages from Scripture, heartfelt sharing of the burden with the Lord in prayer, spiritual reading about the issues involved—all the many spiritual means at our disposal—and the willingness to persevere on this path, will lead to freedom.

21

Nonspiritual Desolation

When John meets with Father Reed (chapter 1), he says:

Now I feel like I just can't pray. It's frustrating. . . . I don't feel God's closeness in the same way. I go to daily Mass because I want to be faithful, but it doesn't energize me the way it used to. I try to pray the Mass, but my mind wanders, and I feel bad about that. And to be honest, I don't really want to pray the Rosary during the commute. Some days I don't. I pray before retiring, but it's simply to get it done. I'm tired, and what I really want is to go to bed and sleep.

John's prayer is dry. He is overly tired, and this weighs on his prayer.

When Beth meets with Father Reed (chapter 2), she shares her discouragement, tells him of her colleague's criticisms, and adds:

This has been going on for a long time, and it wears on me. When I get home after a day like that, I try to pray, but I'm too discouraged. I wind up watching movies or reading the feed on Facebook, getting emptier and more depressed all the time.

Beth's prayer is dry. She is emotionally depleted, and this renders prayer difficult.

∞

When Paul meets with Father Reed (chapter 3), he says:

I get up tired. I don't want to face the day. I don't want to pray or help in the parish. Even being present to my wife and children feels like a burden.... I drag myself to the school, and I'm just glad when the day is over.... My sleep is poor. I'm not exercising.... I can sum it up this way: I'm tired, I'm discouraged, I feel like I can't go on, and I don't see the way out. How do you even pray when you feel like this?

Paul's prayer, too, is dry. He is exhausted, and so finds prayer hard.

∞

Physical and emotional issues (nonspiritual desolation) may also cause dryness in prayer. These may include: excessive physical activity, lack of sleep, dietary questions, allergies, medical concerns, grief, depression, and similar physical and emotional stresses.

Such is the case with John, whose pace of work and lack of sleep cause dryness in prayer; with Beth, whose emotional discouragement also results in dry prayer; and with Paul, whose burnout renders prayer dry. In each case, the dryness results from a depletion of human energy; in each case, therefore, the remedy is wise attention to our human needs.

22

Spiritual Desolation

In the preceding chapter, we examined dryness in prayer arising from *nonspiritual* desolation—that is, physical and emotional depletion. Dryness in prayer, however, may also be a form of *spiritual* desolation. I cite the following from the many examples already seen.

John writes in his journal (chapter 7):

> *Why doesn't prayer bring me peace? Why do I continue to feel agitated?... The feeling is that others find peace through prayer—Jennie seems to—but that I can't. I wonder what's wrong with me. Am I missing something in the spiritual life? Doing something wrong? Why am I struggling like this? Why can't I feel God's closeness? And why, when I so need God and try to pray, do I feel these temptations to turn to the phone, the Internet, social media, even alcohol in ways that I know are harmful? And will I ever get through this? The feeling is that this will just go on.*

John's prayer this day is dry, troubled, and mingled with temptations. This dryness is on the spiritual level: he cannot find peace in prayer, God does not feel close, he is tempted toward "low and earthly things," and he feels that this spiritual state will persist.

∞

Julie tells her friend (chapter 8):

> *I find myself thinking like this: You believed you were growing in love of God. Look at you now. You're not faithful to prayer, you don't get along with your husband, and you don't take good care of your son. You've been fooling yourself. You thought that the retreat was a time of grace, and you thought that God was calling you to grow spiritually. Look at how poorly it's all going. How do you know that was God? How do you know you heard his voice? To judge by the results, you didn't.*

Julie's prayer at this time is dry, despondent, and marked by lack of confidence. Her dryness is on the spiritual level: she doubts her growth in love of God, fears that she is fooling herself in her spiritual life, questions the grace of her retreat, and doubts that God is calling her to growth.

∞

Cathy writes in her journal (chapter 10):

> *Today, I don't feel God's love or compassion. All that warmth I felt in the first weeks – "You are precious.... I love you.... Behind and before you encircle me and rest your hand upon me," – all of that is gone. I wonder if it was even real. I don't feel loved. I feel abandoned. I feel alone. I hurt. I can't go on like this. I want to quit praying. Why should I pray when this happens?*

Cathy's prayer this day is dry, discouraged, and characterized by a sense of isolation. Her dryness, too, is on the spiritual level: she does not feel God's love, the warmth of earlier prayer is gone, she feels alone and abandoned by God, she doubts her former prayer, and she inclines toward stopping prayer altogether.

∽

In speaking of spiritual consolation and spiritual desolation, Ignatius tells us that a person may experience "dryness against tears."[25] That is, in times of spiritual consolation, tears may express the person's joyful awareness of God's love and closeness. In times of spiritual desolation, the contrary may be true: the person may feel spiritually dry, devoid of warm feelings, arid, like a desert without water. An early Jesuit source describes this form of spiritual desolation as "dryness of affect."[26]

When dryness is accompanied by discouragement in the spiritual life, by a feeling of distance from God, by a loss of hope for spiritual growth, by a sense of failure in spiritual efforts, by a lack of energy for spiritual things, or by various temptations—that is, by the forms of spiritual desolation we explored in part 2 of this book—then this dryness is spiritual desolation. Such specifically *spiritual* desolation is evident in the words of John, Julie, and Cathy cited here.

Because the enemy readily works in our human vulnerabilities, healthy nonspiritual steps—exercise, time with friends, sufficient sleep, and the like—render us less susceptible to spiritual desolation.

---

[25] *Monumenta Historica Societatis Iesu*, vol. 76, 72, para. [12]. In the original, "*sequedad contra lágrimas.*"

[26] Ibid., 457, para. [76]. See Gallagher, *Setting Captives Free*, 75–76.

When we do find ourselves in spiritual desolation, spiritual remedies must be employed. We have discussed these above and summarized them in chapter 14: make no changes to your spiritual proposals; turn to prayer of petition, meditation, examination, and suitable penance; remember that you can overcome the desolation with God's grace; consider, too, that it will pass much sooner than the enemy would have you believe; prepare ahead of time when in consolation; resist in the very beginning; speak with a wise and competent spiritual person; identify and strengthen the point of greatest vulnerability. These are good friends for the journey!

Part 4

The Dark Night

23

The Dark Night of the Senses

E-mail to Cathy from a friend, one year after her meeting with Father Reed (chapter 18):

> Hi, Cathy. I want to thank you for helping me with the children last week. I don't know what I would have done without you while I was in the hospital. I have to tell you, I've always appreciated our friendship, but somehow, it's become richer this past year. I've loved seeing the changes in you. You have more peace, and you give me more peace. You notice people who need help and reach out so sensitively, the way you did for us last week. I've seen, too, that since Father asked you to lead the Spiritual Life Commission in the parish, it has a whole new energy. Above all, though, I want to say "Thank you." I'm so grateful to you for helping me in a difficult time.

From Cathy's journal, a week later:

> After a year of warm and blessed prayer, it has gotten harder. I thought I knew how to pray, and I've even given

talks on prayer this past year. But now, I feel like I just can't pray. I don't know what to do. Nothing seems to work. I try to think about the scriptural passage or imagine myself there, and ... nothing. Nothing happens. I wouldn't mind if it were just a day or even a week, but it's all the time now. I can tell others how to pray, but I can't pray anymore.

From Cathy's journal, two weeks later:

I used to look forward to prayer. I don't anymore. There is no warmth or focus. It's just dry, and it seems to be getting worse. For a long time, now, I've loved prayer and spiritual things and found such energy in them. Now all of that seems gone. When I try to pray, I can't think. I can't imagine. I don't know what to do. This can't be good. I wonder if I'm failing the Lord somehow.

From Cathy's journal, ten days later:

What is happening? When I try to pray, it all feels empty, insipid. God is absent. This is not getting better, and it's becoming painful. Lord, you know that I only want you. What is wrong? Why am I regressing? Why don't I feel your closeness anymore? Why does nothing help? Why are you silent?

From Cathy's journal, five days later:

In prayer, everything is dark, everything is painful. It just keeps getting worse. Before I returned to God, I looked for pleasure and consolation in people, places, things I had, travel, and the like. When I turned back to God, I stopped centering my life on these things. God became my focus, and I found a joy that nothing else ever gave me. He was there every time I turned to him, and I loved to pray.

Now, both are gone: I don't want to live for material things as I did before, and I can't. They don't have the same place in my heart anymore. But now, God, too, has abandoned me. I have no joy, no delight, no consolation anywhere, whether in material things or in God. Where can I turn? Lord, why have you left me alone and in pain when you are all I want?

From Cathy's journal, a week later:

I keep thinking about you, Lord, all day long. You are all my heart desires. I don't want anything else. But I can't find you. Everything is empty. There is no taste, no attraction when I pray. I just want to be alone and to be with you, but you are not there. You matter so much to me, and I'm losing you. I can't pray. I don't know what to do. I've never felt pain like this before. Why do you awaken in me such desires for you and then abandon me? I'm so afraid that I will lose everything, that I'll go back to the way I was.

From Cathy's journal, two weeks later:

I'm so confused; my heart is so heavy, I feel so far from God. So I decided to try again the way of praying that has helped in the past, the one Father Bauer taught us, when we think about a biblical passage or imagine ourselves in the scene. And it didn't help. I had to force myself to think about the day's Gospel, but it was like walking into a strong headwind.

I don't want to do it. I can't do it. So I am left with nothing. Lord, I am in pain, in darkness, wanting only you and unable to find you. It's so hard, and I am afraid.

E-mail from Cathy to Father Reed, that evening:

Father, I am really struggling in prayer. I don't know what's happening. Could I speak with you? Thank you, Cathy

E-mail from Father Reed to Cathy, the next day:

Yes, certainly. If that 1:00 p.m. time on Saturday continues to work for you, I'm free then. Blessings and prayers, Father Reed

∞

They met in the parlor, and after a brief prayer, Father Reed prepared to listen. Cathy asked if she could read to him her recent journal entries, and Father Reed agreed.

When Cathy finished, Father Reed thought for a moment. Then, he said, "Cathy, I know how painful this is for you. You've described it well—how it feels like regressing, failing in prayer, and losing God, who is everything for you. I can understand that you are afraid."

Cathy nodded. "Yes," she said, "I am afraid. Everything is dark, and the joy I had before has turned to pain. Can you help me see how I've failed the Lord? Where I've gone wrong and why I've lost the Lord?"

"Cathy, what do you want?"

"I want the Lord! More than ever. All the time. That's why this hurts so much."

"Yes, that is so apparent in you, and it's beautiful."

Father Reed paused and then said, "We'll need to turn to Saint John of the Cross for answers. He is our primary teacher here. He described what you are experiencing in his book *The Dark Night*. This is happening not because you are regressing—your deep desire for God and the way you live shows clearly that you are not. Quite the contrary. It's happening because God is calling you to a new kind of prayer and is preparing you for it. John of the Cross calls this kind of experience a "dark night." You can see how apt the metaphor is."

"Yes, darkness is a good word for it."

"So, the first thing is not to be afraid of what's happening. It's happening because you are growing spiritually, and God wants to bring you still closer to Himself. The call is to go through this faithfully, without fear, confident that God's love is at work in this darkness."

"What does it mean to go through this faithfully? How do you do that?"

"We'll take our answer from John of the Cross again. Don't give up prayer, and don't shorten the time. Be patient with these struggles, and don't be discouraged by them. God is working in you through them, and if you persevere, he will accomplish his purpose in you."

Cathy nodded her understanding.

"Another important thing about your prayer. Don't force yourself to try reflecting on a scriptural passage or imagining yourself in the scene. Your comparison of walking against a strong headwind is a good one. God is no longer asking you to pray that way. Just remain quiet in the prayer, attentive to God. And do this even though you feel nothing, even though you don't sense God's presence. He is there, working silently in your heart, purifying you, preparing you for deeper communion and love. All you need to do when you pray is be present to God. Just be open and attentive to Him. He will do the rest. And be very sure that you are not wasting time when you do this. You are allowing God to work in you, which is all He asks of you now in prayer."

∝∾

Father Reed recognizes that Cathy's experience is the "dark night of the senses" described by John of the Cross.[27] She does not exaggerate when she writes, "*In prayer, everything is dark, everything is painful*" and describes the fear, anxiety, and distance from God she feels. John himself describes this night as "bitter" (*amarga*) and "terrible" (*terrible*).[28]

That Cathy experiences this night reveals not regression but, rather, rich spiritual growth. External signs confirm this, as her friend indicates in her e-mail. Through this dark night, God purifies Cathy and prepares her for a new kind of prayer, less active, more receptive, that which John of the Cross calls contemplation. In such contemplation, God simply pours himself, his love, and his grace into the human heart. The call, as Father Reed says to Cathy, is to be attentive, quiet, present, and to allow God to do this. "For," John says, "contemplation is nothing else than a secret

---

[27] In this and the following chapter, I explore John of the Cross's two passive dark nights: the dark night of the senses and the dark night of the spirit. These are passive in that God works in the person, and the person's call is to receive this work, to allow God to accomplish his or her purification through it. In addition to the two passive nights, John also speaks of two corresponding active nights, that of the senses and that of the spirit. In these, the person actively pursues purification.

[28] *The Dark Night*, 1, 8, 2, in *The Collected Works of Saint John of the Cross*, ed. Kieran Kavanaugh, OCD, and Otilio Rodriguez, OCD (Washington, DC: ICS Publications, 1991), 376.

and peaceful and loving inflow of God, which, if not hampered, fires the soul in the spirit of love."[29]

We must also note the great difference between the dark night and spiritual desolation. The first is a work of God; the second, a work of the enemy. The first purifies and prepares a person for growth in prayer; the second, if not resisted, harms the person. The first is caused by love and leads to love; the second is a discouraging lie. The first is to be understood and accepted; the second is to be understood and rejected.

John of the Cross indicates that one who experiences the dark night of the senses will need help to understand it. With sure intuition, Cathy recognizes this need and speaks with Father Reed. Without such help, the person may grow discouraged and fail to persevere. Because this is a sensitive spiritual experience, the person will need a wise and competent spiritual director, one experienced and learned enough to recognize the dark night of the senses. Should questions like Cathy's arise in your prayer, do not remain alone with them. Seek a competent spiritual director and speak about your experience.

---

[29] *The Dark Night*, 1, 10, 6, in *Collected Works*, 382.

24

The Dark Night of the Spirit

A final trial, the most painful and the most blessed, may be experienced in the spiritual life. We will explore this through the example of a saint, Teresa of Calcutta. This trial John of the Cross calls "the dark night of the spirit."[30]

Like the dark night of the senses, the dark night of the spirit is a work of God. Through this darkness, a person is radically purified and prepared for the highest communion with God possible in this life.

In this night, God works, and the person receives his purifying action. John describes it as follows: "This dark night is an inflow of God into the soul, which purges it of its habitual ignorances and imperfections, natural and spiritual."[31] The dark night of the spirit, one author comments, "is constituted by a series of passive purgations that are extremely painful and have for their object the completion of the purification that was begun but not completed by the night of the senses. By means of the terrifying trials of this second night, the defects of the soul are uprooted at

---

[30] See *The Dark Night*, bk. 2.
[31] *The Dark Night*, 2, 5, 1, in *Collected Works*, 401.

their very source, something that could not be accomplished by the purification of the senses."[32]

John compares this dark night of the spirit to fire that burns wood. When applied to wood, fire first removes from it all moisture, all impurities, and blackens it. Then the fire "transforms the wood into itself and makes it as beautiful as it is itself."[33]

As in the dark night of the senses, the person's call is to bear this night faithfully and allow God to do his purifying work.

The intensity of this night is evident in Saint Teresa of Calcutta's experience of it. When Teresa shared her experience with her spiritual director, Father Joseph Neuner, SJ, he wrote:

> My answer to the confession of these pages was simple: there was no indication of any serious failure on her part which could explain the spiritual dryness. It was simply the dark night of which all masters of spiritual life know—though I never found it so deeply and for so many years as in her. There is no human remedy against it. It can be borne only in the assurance of God's hidden presence and of the union with Jesus who in His passion had to bear the burden and darkness of the sinful world for our salvation. The sure sign of God's hidden presence in this darkness in the thirst for God, the craving for at least a ray of His light. No one can long for God unless God is present

---

[32] Jordan Aumann, OP, *Spiritual Theology* (London: Sheed and Ward, 1980), 203.

[33] *The Dark Night*, 2, 10, 1, in *Collected Works*, 416.

in his/her heart. *Thus the only response to this trial is the total surrender to God and the acceptance of the darkness in union with Jesus.*[34]

Aware that we are on holy ground, we will approach Teresa's experience with great reverence. Her life witnesses both to the profound darkness of this night and to its astounding fruitfulness. The style and punctuation in the following quotations is Teresa's own.

On July 3, 1959, the saint wrote:

> *Lord, my God, who am I that You should forsake me? The child of Your love – and now become as the most hated one – the one You have thrown away as unwanted – unloved. I call, I cling, I want – and there is no One to answer – no One on Whom I can cling – no, No One. – Alone. The darkness is so dark – and I am alone. – Unwanted, forsaken. – The loneliness of the heart that wants love is unbearable – Where is my faith? Even deep down, right in, there is nothing but emptiness & and darkness. – My God – how painful is this unknown pain....*
>
> *The whole time smiling. – Sisters & people pass such remarks. – They think my faith, trust & love are filling my very being & that the intimacy with God and union to His will must be absorbing my heart. – Could they but know – and how my cheerfulness is the cloak by which I cover the emptiness & misery.*[35]

[34] Brian Kolodiejchuk, MC, ed., *Mother Teresa: Come Be My Light* (New York: Image, 2007), 214.

[35] Ibid., 187.

Struggles in the Spiritual Life

Three months later, on September 3, 1959:

> In my heart there is no faith – no love – no trust – there is
> so much pain – the pain of longing, the pain of not being
> wanted. – I want God with all the powers of my soul – and
> yet there between us – there is terrible separation. – I don't
> pray any longer – I utter words of community prayers – and
> try my utmost to get out of every word the sweetness it has
> to give. – But my prayer of union is not there any longer. – I
> no longer pray. – My soul is not one with You – and yet when
> alone in the streets – I talk to you for hours – of my longing
> for You. – How intimate are those words – and yet so empty,
> for they leave me far from You.

The saint describes her response:

> Jesus hear my prayer – if this pleases You – if my pain
> and suffering – my darkness and separation gives You a
> drop of consolation – my own Jesus, do with me as You
> wish – as long as You wish, without a single glance at my
> feelings and pain. I am Your own. – Imprint on my soul
> and life the sufferings of Your Heart. Don't mind my feel-
> ings. – Don't mind even, my pain. If my separation from
> You – brings others to You and in their love and company
> You find joy and pleasure – why Jesus, I am willing with
> all my heart to suffer all that I suffer – not only now – but
> for all eternity – if this was possible. Your happiness is all
> that I want.[36]

[36] Ibid., 193-194.

The signs of John's dark night of the spirit are here: a mature person, loving, dedicated, long united to God in deep prayer, a life of faithful and fruitful service, a smile, complete openness to God's will—and utter, painful spiritual darkness. Teresa senses that her interior suffering brings others to God, gives God joy. And his happiness is all she desires.

A year and a half later, in April 1961:

> *Since 49 or 50 [1949 or 1950] this terrible sense of loss—this untold darkness—this loneliness—this continual longing for God—which gives me that pain deep down in my heart.—Darkness is such that I really do not see—neither with my mind nor with my reason.—The place of God in my soul is blank.—There is no God in me.—When the pain of longing is so great—I just long & long for God—and then it is that I feel—He does not want me—He is not here—Heaven—souls—why these are just words—which mean nothing to me.—My very life seems so contradictory. I help souls—to go where?—Why all this? Where is the soul in my very being? God does not want ne.—Sometimes—I just hear my own heart cry out—"My God" and nothing else comes—The torture and pain I can't explain....*
>
> *You see, Father, the contradiction in my life. I long for God—I want to love Him—to love Him much—to live only for love of Him—to love only—and yet there is but pain—longing and no love....*
>
> *Before I could spend hours before Our Lord—loving Him—talking to Him—and now—not even meditation goes properly—nothing but "My God"—even that sometimes does not come.—Yet deep down somewhere in my heart that longing for God keeps breaking through the darkness. When*

outside – in the work – or meeting people – there is a pres-
ence – of somebody living very close – in very me. – I don't
know what this is – but very often, even every day – that love
in me for God grows more real. – I find myself telling Jesus
unconsciously most strange tokens of love.[37]

It would be difficult to find a greater instance and a more complete description of John's dark night of the spirit.

Spiritual writers such as Dominican Father Réginald Garrigou-Lagrange suggest that, in some cases, God may prolong the dark night even when it has already purified the person. In this case, the night serves "to make the already purified soul work for the salvation of its neighbor."[38] In this sense, we can understand the long duration of Teresa's dark night. Seldom, if ever, did anyone do more for her neighbor than Saint Teresa of Calcutta. Her life and witness blessed and continue to bless the whole world.

The first night, that of the senses, John writes, is "bitter and terrible." But, he continues, "nothing can be compared to the second, for it is horrible and frightful to the spirit."[39] Horrible (*horrenda*) and frightful (*espantable*): Teresa's experience verifies this in full. A person utterly, deeply, totally in love with God, habituated to loving communion with Him, dedicated to his service – now bereft of him, unable to find him, feeling abandoned by him, unwanted. The fire is purifying the wood, preparing the deepest union with God the human heart can know in this life and rendering the person profoundly fruitful in the service of the Lord.

[37] Ibid., 210–211.
[38] Cited in ibid., 382, no. 16.
[39] *The Dark Night*, 1, 8, 2, in *Collected Works*, 376.

Those who undergo this night will benefit from wise and competent spiritual direction. Having faithfully endured the darkness, they will experience its blessed fruits. Fire, John says in the passage quoted, "transforms the wood into itself and makes it as beautiful as it is itself."

Conclusion

The day was August 8, 1897, the month before her death.[40] Thérèse lay on her sickbed. Her sister Pauline was with her in the room. As she lay there, Thérèse pondered her life. In particular, she remembered the Christmas night eleven years earlier when she received what she had called "the grace of my complete conversion."[41] On that "night of light,"[42] God's grace and an act of courage liberated her from the nervousness and sensitivity that had oppressed her for years. Thérèse thought, too, of Judith in the Old Testament and of the courage with which she had acted.

Thérèse began to speak. Many, she told her sister, feel that they lack such courage. Then she said, "God never refuses that first grace that gives one the courage to act; afterwards, the heart is strengthened, and one advances from victory to victory."[43]

---

[40] For this incident, see St. Thérèse of Lisieux: Her Last Conversations, ed. John Clarke, OCD (Washington, DC: ICS Publications, 1977), 142.

[41] Story of a Soul: The Autobiography of Saint Thérèse of Lisieux, trans. John Clarke, OCD (Washington, DC: ICS Publications, 1996), 98.

[42] Story of a Soul, 98.

[43] Last Conversations, 142.

That is the message of this book. A path to liberation from discouragement, confusion, and pain in the spiritual life exists. God has not called us to captivity but to freedom. Clarity regarding the struggle is possible, and remedies are available. Begin. Take the first step. Take it now. And take it knowing that "God never refuses that first grace that gives one the courage to act; afterwards, the heart is strengthened, and one advances from victory to victory." May that grace and that courage bless our spiritual lives.

Saint Ignatius's 14 Rules for Discernment: Contemporary Version

1. When a person lives a life of serious sin, the enemy fills the imagination with images of sensual pleasures; the good spirit stings and bites in the person's conscience, God's loving action, calling the person back.
2. When a person tries to avoid sin and to love God, this reverses: now the enemy tries to bite, discourage, and sadden; the good spirit gives courage and strength, inspirations, easing the path forward.
3. When your heart finds joy in God, a sense of God's closeness and love, you are experiencing spiritual consolation. Open your heart to God's gift!
4. When your heart is discouraged, you have little energy for spiritual things, and God feels far away, you are experiencing spiritual desolation. Resist and reject this tactic of enemy!
5. "In time of desolation, never make a change!" When you are in spiritual desolation, never change anything in your spiritual life.

6. When you are in spiritual desolation, use these four means: prayer (ask God's help!), meditation (think of Bible verses, truths about God's faithful love, memories of God's fidelity to you in the past), examination (ask: What am I feeling? How did this start?), and suitable penance (don't give in and don't immerse yourself in social media, music, movies, and so forth). Stand your ground in suitable ways!

7. When you are in spiritual desolation, think of this truth: God is giving me all the grace I need to get safely through this desolation.

8. When you are in spiritual desolation, be patient, stay the course, and remember that consolation will return much sooner than the desolation is telling you.

9. Why does a God who loves us allow us to experience spiritual desolation? To help us see changes we need to make; to strengthen us in our resistance to desolation; and to help us not grow complacent in the spiritual life.

10. When you are in spiritual consolation, remember that desolation will return at some point, and prepare for it.

11. Strive to be a mature person of discernment: neither carelessly high in consolation nor despairingly low in desolation, but humble in consolation and trusting in desolation.

12. Resist the enemy's temptations right at their very beginning. This is when it is easiest.

13. When you find burdens on your heart in your spiritual life—temptations, confusion, discouragement—find a wise, competent spiritual person, and talk about it.

14. Identify that area of your life where you are most vulnerable to the enemy's temptations and discouraging lies, and strengthen it.[44]

---

[44] Published in Timothy Gallagher, OMV, *Discernment of Spirits in Marriage: Ignatian Wisdom for Husbands and Wives* (Manchester, NH: Sophia Institute Press, 2020), 145–147.

Resources

Books

The Discernment of Spirits: An Ignatian Guide to Everyday Living (New York: Crossroad, 2005)

When You Struggle in the Spiritual Life: An Ignatian Path to Freedom (New York: Crossroad, 2021)

Discernment of Spirits in Marriage: Ignatian Wisdom for Husbands and Wives (Manchester, NH: Sophia Institute Press, 2020)

Overcoming Spiritual Discouragement: The Wisdom and Spiritual Power of Venerable Bruno Lanteri (Irondale, AL: EWTN, 2019)

Podcasts

Father Gallagher's podcast series on: DiscerningHearts.com and on the Discerning Heart app

For further materials: frtimothygallagher.org

About the Author

Father Timothy M. Gallagher, OMV, was ordained in 1979 as a member of the Oblates of the Virgin Mary, a religious community dedicated to giving retreats and spiritual formation according to the Spiritual Exercises of Saint Ignatius. Having obtained his doctorate in 1983 from the Gregorian University, he has taught (Saint John's Seminary, Brighton, Massachusetts; Our Lady of Grace Seminary Residence, Boston), assisted in formation work, and served two terms as provincial in his community. He is a frequent speaker on EWTN, and his digitally recorded talks are used around the world. He has written ten books on Ignatian discernment and prayer and several books on Venerable Bruno Lanteri and the Liturgy of the Hours. He currently holds the Saint Ignatius Chair for Spiritual Formation at Saint John Vianney Theological Seminary in Denver.

Sophia Institute

Sophia Institute is a nonprofit institution that seeks to nurture the spiritual, moral, and cultural life of souls and to spread the Gospel of Christ in conformity with the authentic teachings of the Roman Catholic Church.

Sophia Institute Press fulfills this mission by offering translations, reprints, and new publications that afford readers a rich source of the enduring wisdom of mankind.

Sophia Institute also operates the popular online resource CatholicExchange.com. *Catholic Exchange* provides world news from a Catholic perspective as well as daily devotionals and articles that will help readers to grow in holiness and live a life consistent with the teachings of the Church.

In 2013, Sophia Institute launched Sophia Institute for Teachers to renew and rebuild Catholic culture through service to Catholic education. With the goal of nurturing the spiritual, moral, and cultural life of souls, and an abiding respect for the role and work of teachers, we strive to provide materials and programs that are at once enlightening to the mind and ennobling to the heart; faithful and complete, as well as useful and practical.

Sophia Institute gratefully recognizes the Solidarity Association for preserving and encouraging the growth of our apostolate over the course of many years. Without their generous and timely support, this book would not be in your hands.

www.SophiaInstitute.com
www.CatholicExchange.com
www.SophiaInstituteforTeachers.org

Sophia Institute Press® is a registered trademark of Sophia Institute.
Sophia Institute is a tax-exempt institution as defined by the
Internal Revenue Code, Section 501(c)(3). Tax ID 22-2548708.